Bulletin Boards & Displays

grade

Student-Centered Displays

- Reinforce the curriculum
- Showcase student work
- Help manage classroom routines
- Create a positive learning environment
- Help motivate students

Use throughout the year!

Managing Editor: Gerri Primak

Editorial Team: Becky S. Andrews, Kimberley Bruck, Sharon Murphy, Debra Liverman, Diane Badden, Thad H. McLaurin, Jenny Chapman, Lynn Drolet, Karen A. Brudnak, Juli Docimo Blair, Hope Rodgers, Dorothy C. McKinney, Stephanie Affinito, Karen Almond, Carol Alvarnaz, Randi Austin, Pamela Ballingall, Susan Bango, Cindy Barber, Jean Berger, Jenny Berry, Melissa Bickley, Janet Boyce, Suzanne Bright, Andrea Bucholz, Melissa Burke, Jill Carswell, Yvonne Clark, Patricia Dentinger, Marilyn Dickson, Tina Ellis, Jean Eppler, Pamela Frey, Amy Fritz, Ada Goren, Stacey Harper, Debbie Hill, Katy Hoh, Nancy House, Theresa Jones, Alison LaMana, Erika Laport, Joy Lumley, Kristen McDowell, Kristin Miller, Marie O'Neill, Dawn Pinson, Julia Portnoy, Alesia Richards, Anna Robinson, Marline Schindewolf, Stephanie Sisson, Pam Smith, Kristy Spradlin, Heather Sukow, Joyce Sutherland, Norma Sween, Susan Walker, Kathleen Washington, Joyce Wilson, Patricia Woods, Clair Zaffaroni, Sara Zimdars

Production Team: Lori Z. Henry, Pam Crane, Rebecca Saunders, Chris Curry, Sarah Foreman, Theresa Lewis Goode, Greg D. Rieves, Eliseo De Jesus Santos II, Barry Slate, Donna K. Teal, Zane Williard, Tazmen Carlisle, Kathy Coop, Marsha Heim, Lynette Dickerson, Mark Rainey

www.themailbox.com

©2007 The Mailbox®
All rights reserved.
ISBN10 #1-56234-763-2 • ISBN13 #978-156234-763-5

Manufactured in the United States
10 9 8 7 6 5 4 3 2 1

Table of Contents

Skills Grid

	Back-to-School 	Fall	Winter 	Spring	End of the Year	Anytime
Listening and Speaking						
making introductions	10, 11					
sharing information			38			
Literacy						
alphabetical order	10	22		42		
descriptive words			26			
fact and opinion				48		
letter writing						59
name recognition	8					
nouns		23				59
opposites				44		
punctuation				48		
reading motivation	9, 14	20, 22	32	40		68
reference skills						60
rhyming		17				
spelling			29			68
synonyms			36	49		
vocabulary		16	26	42	55	
word families				47		57
writing	7, 14	15, 16, 19, 23	26, 30, 33, 34, 35	40, 42, 43, 46, 49	52, 54, 55, 56	58, 60, 61, 65, 73
Math						
addition		21	36	41		62, 63
attributes						60, 73
comparing sets			27			
counting backward					51	
counting by fives						61
fact families			36			
glyphs		19	32, 101			
graphing	10, 12	24			55	
measurement		20		44		
money			36	45		
ordinal numbers				44		
skill review		24	25			63
subtraction						63
symmetry				43		
Science and Health						
dental health			37			
nutrition						73
vocabulary						63
Social Studies						
Black History Month			38			
Constitution Day		17				
map skills	12					
Presidents' Day			37			
traditions			27, 30			
transportation					55	

Quick Tips

A Hands-On Display

Cover a trifold board with colorful paper for a portable interactive display! This display board is great for manipulative centers, attendance displays, and management displays. Not only is the board the perfect height for students, it is also easy to store!

See page 72 for this bulletin board idea!

Ready-to-Go Lettering

Decorative Con-Tact paper is perfect for making letters for your bulletin boards. Once each letter is cut, simply peel the backing off and stick it to the board!

Write-On Boards

Cover any bulletin board surface with clear Con-Tact paper, and you have an instant wipe-off board! Students can write directly on the board and then wipe off their work with a damp cloth.

Beautiful Backgrounds

Instead of using bulletin board paper to cover a board, try these reusable materials!

- plastic tablecloths

- fabric

- sheets of felt

- twin-size bedsheets

Back-to-School

Blast into a new year of activities with an out-of-this-world welcome! Color an enlarged copy of the rocket pattern on page 74 and program it with a title. Then label planet cutouts (pattern on page 74) with different school activities. Arrange the rocket, the planets, and adhesive foil stars on a board. On the first day of school, give each youngster a copy of the rocket pattern to personalize, color, and cut out. Then add the completed rockets to the display.

This underwater scene isn't complete without student-made fish! Substitute a large paper plate in the directions below and make a teacher fish. Post the fish and some twisted blue and green crepe paper (seaweed) on a board. Then have each child make a fish (see below) to complete the display.

"Fin-tastic" Fish

Supplies:
small paper plate
scissors
glue
markers

Steps:
1. Cut a triangle from the paper plate to create a mouth.
2. Glue the triangle to the plate so that it resembles a fish tail.
3. Write your name on the fish.
4. Embellish with details as desired.

Waking Up to a New School Year

Ms. Sutherland

Try this quilted display of student favorites! Cut two long rectangles so they resemble bedposts and top each one with a large circle. Have each student draw or write on a construction paper square something she likes to do at school. Then hole-punch the squares and thread them with yarn so they resemble a quilt. Write your name on a construction paper pillow and arrange the completed pieces as shown.

Add student-made strawberries to this patch for a sweet display! Twist green raffia to create vines. Assemble the vines on a bulletin board so they resemble a strawberry patch. Title the board with a welcome sign. Give each student a copy of a berry pattern on page 118. Have him color, cut out, and personalize the berry. Finally, attach each completed berry to the patch.

Have each youngster draw a picture of herself on a sheet of paper. Post each portrait with a corresponding student photograph for youngsters to compare and contrast. After a desired amount of time, send the keepsakes home to serve as a lasting reminder of the first few days of first grade!

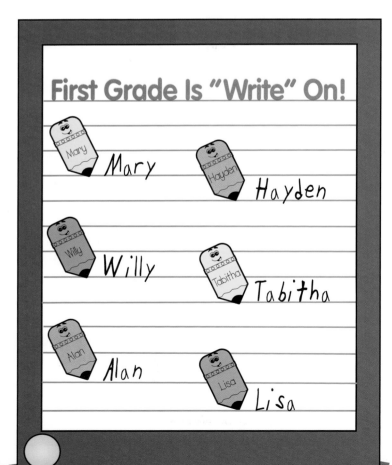

Student names are the main attraction of this door display. For each student, program a pencil cutout (pattern on page 75) with his name. Glue the pencils to a sheet of chart paper that will fit on your door. Have each youngster, in turn, find his pencil and then write his name next to it. Post the resulting autographed notebook paper on the door to showcase your sharp students!

"WHOOOO'S" in Ms. Lumley's Class?

Georgio
Jeanette
Isabella
Amaya
Chris
Jazmin
Terrell
Vera

Not only will this scene help youngsters feel welcome, but it is also ready-to-go to showcase student work! Color and cut out an enlarged copy of the owl pattern on page 76. Write each student's name on an individual paper star. Arrange the pieces under a title. During the first week of school, invite each child to choose a favorite piece of work to display with his star.

Use the owl cutout again. See page 24.

✱ Variations

- **"Whoooo" Is Reading?**
  Have each student draw or write about a favorite story or book. Display his completed paper by his star.

- **"Whoooo" Has Good Behavior?**
  At the end of each day, post a thin strip of paper (ray) by a child's star if she demonstrated acceptable behavior. When a child's star has a desired number of rays, reward her with a note home, a trip to your prize basket, or a similar treat.

- **"Whoooo" Is Thankful?**
  Use the owl cutout for a Thanksgiving display. Have each youngster draw or write about things that he is thankful for. Display each youngster's work by his star.

Lining Up for a Great School Year

Here's a lineup that is sure to help students get to know one another. Give each youngster a copy of the T-shirt pattern on page 77. Have her share something about herself by drawing or writing on the shirt. When she is satisfied with her work, instruct her to cut out the shirt and hang it on the clothesline. Finally, encourage youngsters to share the information on their shirts.

✔ Student Activities

- **Graphing:** Lead youngsters to recognize common interests on the shirts and graph the results.

- **Alphabetical order:** Transform the display into an interactive lesson by removing the shirts from the line and having youngsters hang them in alphabetical order.

- **Attendance:** Have a helper place the shirts in a laundry basket at the end of each day. In the morning, encourage each youngster to announce his presence by hanging his shirt on the line.

Who Am I?

Program a copy of the owl pattern on page 76 with clues similar to the ones shown. Have each student complete a copy of the programmed owl, color it, and cut it out. While students are out of the room, staple the top of each completed owl to a board. Then post a photo of each student underneath her owl. When time permits, help youngsters read the clues and guess who is hiding behind each owl!

Any magnetic surface is perfect for this attendance display. Give each youngster a person cutout (patterns on page 78) with his name on it. Then have him color the cutout to create a self-likeness. Attach a magnet to the back of each completed cutout. Divide a magnetic surface into two parts and attach the cutouts to one section. Each morning, have each student announce his arrival by moving his cutout to the designated section of the display. A quick glance at the display lets you know who is not at school!

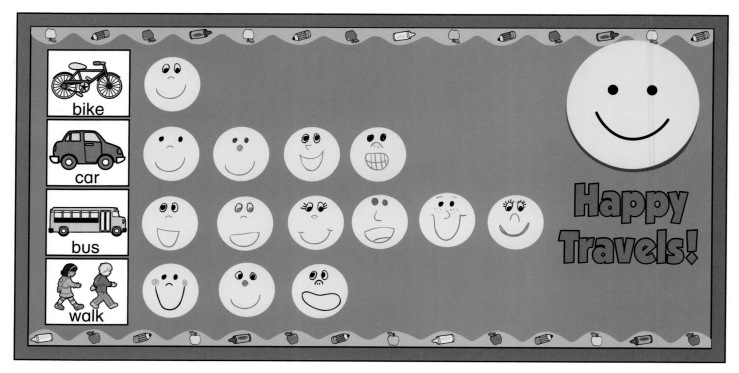

What method of transportation do your youngsters use to get to school? Find out with this travel display! Post on a board a copy of the travel cards on page 79. Then have each youngster draw a smiley face on a four-inch circle. Help each child post his smiley face in the row that shows how he gets to school. Lead youngsters in using the resulting graph to compare and contrast student modes of travel.

Where in the World Have You Been?

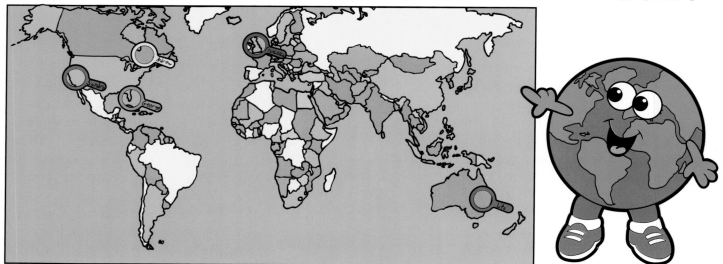

Display an enlarged copy of the globe character pattern on page 80 by a large map. Have each student write her name on a copy of the magnifying glass pattern on page 75. If desired, cut away the inside portion of the magnifying glass and laminate the glass to make it look authentic. Invite each student, in turn, to tell about a place she visited during the summer. Then post her magnifying glass around the area described to create a geographical reference.

Write the name of each month on a different-colored construction paper strip. Then cut out a copy of the balloon pattern on page 81 for each student in the same color as his birthday month. Program each student's balloon with his name and birthday. Then have each youngster add details and attach a length of curled ribbon. Arrange the balloons in a bunch, grouping them by months within the bunch. Each month, post the color-coded month strip and have youngsters find the balloons with the matching color to identify the students who will be celebrating their birthdays!

September

Francis
February 18

Lexi
February 20

Julio
May 23

Fred
August 10

Janet
September 12

Thomas
September 15

Tia
October 6

Peter
November 3

Wheel of Helpers

Marcus — Line Leader
Maria — Homework Helper
Lulu — Attendance Taker
Hannah — Pet Patrol
Tariq — Paper Passer
Kaylee — Lunch Count
Josh — Caboose
Darien — Teacher's Helper

Change classroom jobs quickly with this Ferris wheel display! Draw lines to divide a large circle so there is one section per classroom job. Then program a Ferris wheel seat cutout (patterns on page 82) with the name of each classroom job. Glue the seat pattern to the circle to create a pocket. Next, have each student write her name across the top of a 3" x 5" card and draw a picture of herself below it. To assign jobs, simply place a card in each pocket.

Reach for the Stars!

Motivate youngsters to work toward just about any team goal! Post markers along the side of a display and add several star cutouts. Then attach a copy of the hot-air balloon pattern on page 83 at the bottom of the display. When youngsters demonstrate an established goal, such as walking quietly in line, move the hot-air balloon up to the next marker. When the balloon reaches the top marker, be sure to reward youngsters as desired.

 Variations

- **Soaring With Good News!**
  Give each youngster a copy of the hot-air balloon pattern on page 83. Have him write or draw on the hot-air balloon news he would like to share. Then have him color and cut out the balloon to add to the display.

- **Riding High With Reading!**
  Each time you read a story aloud, make a tally mark on a hot-air balloon cutout. After reading a preselected number of books, move the balloon up to the next marker. Continue in this manner for reading to reach the stars!

For more year-round displays, be sure to check out the "Anytime" section beginning on page 57!

14

Fall

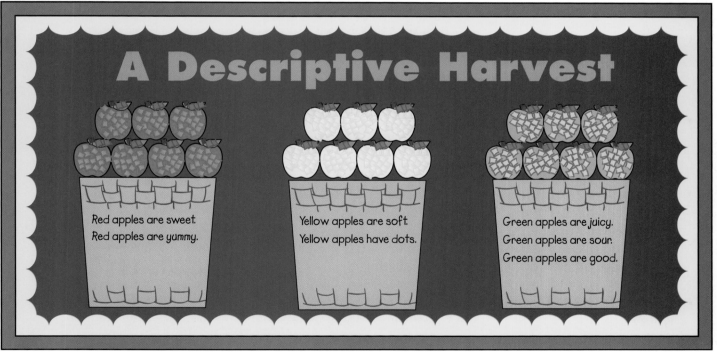

A Descriptive Harvest

Red apples are sweet.
Red apples are yummy.

Yellow apples are soft.
Yellow apples have dots.

Green apples are juicy.
Green apples are sour.
Green apples are good.

Post three basket cutouts on a board. Have each student taste a piece of a yellow apple, a red apple, and a green apple. Then have her color an apple cutout (pattern on page 84) to match her favorite apple. Instruct her to glue to the apple crumpled tissue paper pieces in the corresponding color. Next, sort the apples by color and arrange them over the baskets. Then invite students to dictate descriptive sentences about their apples as you write their words on the corresponding basket.

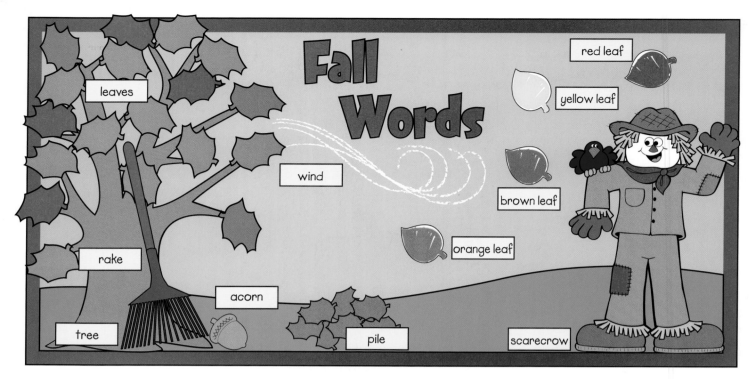

This simple display encourages reading and writing during the fall season. Have students help you create a fall scene on a board. If desired, use selected fall-themed patterns from pages 84–93. Attach word cards and a title. Encourage youngsters to read the words and use them when they write.

✔ Student Activities

- **Writing:** Have a student choose a word from the board and use it in a complete sentence. Then have her illustrate her thoughts.

- **Writing to a prompt:** Have a student choose and respond to a prompt such as one of the following:
    Fall is a colorful time.
    Making piles of leaves is lots of fun!
    Animals gather food to prepare for winter.

- **Writing with color words:** Have each youngster write about three colored items a leaf might pass while blowing in the wind. Then invite him to illustrate his writing.

Encourage pairs of students to work together to name a group of words that rhyme. Have the twosome write and illustrate each word on a separate acorn cutout (pattern on page 84). Display each set of acorns and an enlarged copy of the squirrel pattern on page 85 for a rhyming reference.

Constitution Day (September 17) is a great time of year to display patriotic symbols. Give each student a copy of a United States symbol card (page 86) and help her write about it. Then have her glue the card and her writing to a sheet of construction paper. If desired, have her embellish her paper with star stickers. Finally, post the completed work for a great USA display!

This terrific tiger can accompany excellent work all year long! Color and cut out an enlarged copy of the tiger pattern on page 87. For fall, give each student a copy of the leaf pattern on page 88. Have him write his name on the leaf, color it, and cut it out. Then post the completed leaves and the prepared tiger on a board. Finally, showcase each student's outstanding work by his leaf.

Variations

- **Winter Is "Grrrr-eat"!**
  Have each youngster personalize, color, and cut out a copy of the snowflake pattern on page 88. Post each snowflake with the corresponding student's wonderful work.

- **Spring Is "Grrr-eat"!**
  Have each youngster personalize, color, and cut out a copy of the flower pattern on page 88. Post each flower with the corresponding student's fabulous work.

- **First Grade Is "Grrr-eat"!**
  Have each youngster personalize, color, and cut out a copy of the pawprint pattern on page 88. Post each pawprint with the corresponding student's first-rate work.

OUR PUMPKIN PATCH

Glyph Key

Stem		Teeth	
	I am a girl.		I have lost a tooth.
	I am a boy.		I have not lost a tooth.
Eyes		**Nose**	
●	I like spooky stories.	▲	I have been to a pumpkin patch.
⊙	I do not like spooky stories.	▲	I have not been to a pumpkin patch.

Try this pumpkin glyph activity to create a meaningful wall display! Post a glyph key similar to the one shown. Then have each youngster color a copy of the pumpkin pattern on page 89 according to the key. Arrange the cutout pumpkins and the glyph key on a wall to display details about your youngsters.

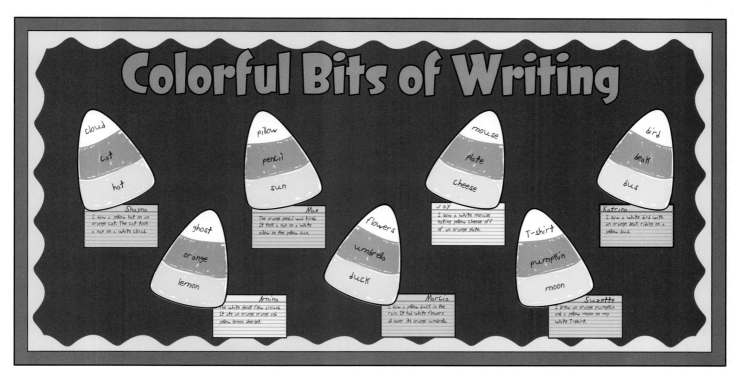

Colorful Bits of Writing

These colorful candies are sure to prompt descriptive writing. Have each youngster color a rounded triangle so it resembles a piece of candy corn. Then help him label each layer with an object of the corresponding color. Encourage him to use his project to write and illustrate a silly scenario that includes all three objects. Finally, post the completed candy corn and accompanying writing on a board.

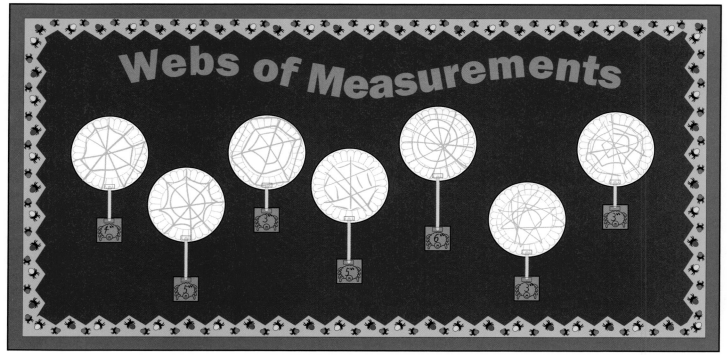

How far down do these spiders dangle? Ask your first graders! Cut three, four, five, or six inches of yarn (dragline) for each student. Have each youngster color a paper plate so it resembles a spiderweb. Then instruct her to measure a dragline and write its length on a copy of a spider card on page 90. Next, have her tape one end of the dragline to her card and the other end to the web. Post the completed projects for a display of wonderful webs!

These batty book reviews display students' favorite stories! Give each child a copy of the bat patterns on page 91. Help him write his name and the title and author of a book on the indicated wing. Then have him complete the sentence on the other wing and illustrate his writing on the bat's body. After he has glued the wings to the body and the glue has dried, attach the bat to a bulletin board. If desired, gently fold the wings forward to create a 3-D display.

Scarecrow Math

Have each child assemble a scarecrow (see below). Then direct her to decorate five one-inch paper squares to create patches. Have the youngster glue each patch on either the scarecrow's shirt or its pants. Next, have her write the corresponding number sentence on the hat. Post the sum on a sun cutout along with the scarecrows for a mathematical display!

Scarecrow

Supplies:
copy of the scarecrow clothes patterns on page 92
3" paper circle
yarn
markers
scissors
glue

Steps:
1. Color and cut out the scarecrow patterns.
2. Glue the cutouts and circle (head) together to make a scarecrow.
3. Add facial details and yarn (hair) to the head as desired.

Reading Road

Celebrate National Children's Book Week with this motivational display! Personalize a car cutout (pattern on page 93) for each student. Arrange the cars on a paper road. Then encourage each youngster to read a book at home each night with a family member. For each book read, have her place a star sticker on her car. Now that's a road to success!

✳ Variations

- **ABC Road**
  Attach the hook side of a Velcro fastener along the road for each car and a loop side to the back of each car. Invite small groups of youngsters to place the cars on the road in alphabetical order.

- **On the Road to Learning!**
  Post incremental steps to a class goal on signs similar to mile markers along the paper road. Then reward achievement by moving a car cutout along your road to success!

- **Reading Races**
  Promote group effort with these cars. Place a car cutout, programmed with names of group members, at the beginning of the road for each small group. Post predetermined goals along the road. Each time a group meets the next posted goal, move the car forward!

Thanksgiving Recipes

Potatoes
Wash them, cut them, and put them in water on the stove. Wait a long time. Dump the water. Serve.

Mashed Potatoes
First, wash some potatoes and put them in a pot. Boil them to make them soft. Add lots of butter and milk. Mush until they are smooth. Eat!

Turkey
Clean it. Add pepper and juice. Put it in the oven all day.

Sweet Potatoes
Cook some on the stove. Smash them up. Spread them in a pan. Add brown stuff and marshmallows on top. Put them in the oven.

Beans
Open can. Dump in pot. Heat. Stir.

Turkey
Get it at a store. Take things out of it. Put it in a really big pot in the oven for a really long time. When it pops, it's done.

Stuffing
Boil water and butter. Add crumbs. Wait. Stir.

These recipes are sure to capture students' attention! Have each youngster write how to prepare a Thanksgiving Day food on a paper that resembles a recipe card. Post each completed card and a title on a bulletin board. When time permits, read a recipe (omitting the title) and have youngsters tell what tasty treat the recipe describes.

We Are Thankful

places

people and animals

things

Give each youngster a yellow, an orange, and a red feather cutout. Then designate each color to represent a person or animal, place, or thing (nouns). Have each student write or draw whom or what he is thankful for on the feathers of the corresponding colors. Finally, arrange the completed feathers around an enlarged copy of the turkey pattern on page 93.

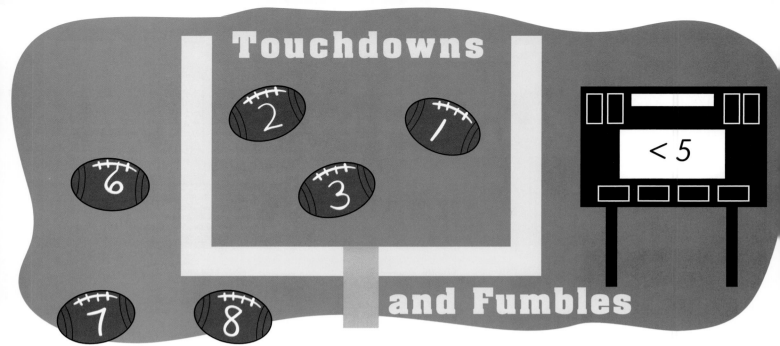

Mount bulletin board paper so it resembles a football goalpost and a scoreboard. Program a class supply of football cutouts with different numbers from 0 to 10. Then write a math skill on a card and secure it to the scoreboard. Have youngsters place footballs with numbers that make true statements inside the goalpost (touchdowns) and numbered footballs that make false statements outside the goalpost (fumbles). To practice a different skill, simply change the card on the scoreboard.

Find out youngsters' favorite holiday pies with a graph display! Post on a board an enlarged copy of the owl pattern on page 76, a graph title, and several different-colored cards labeled with different pie flavors. Have each child write his name on a pie cutout, choose his favorite pie flavor from the board, and color his cutout accordingly. In turn, invite each child to attach his pie to the corresponding column of the graph. Once the graph is complete, discuss the results.

Use the owl cutout again. See page 9.

Winter

Snowball Math

4 + 1 + 3

8 + 0   2 + 6

3 + 5   7 + 1   1 + 5 + 2

8

6 + 1 + 1

4 − 1   5 + 3

4 + 4   10 − 2   2 + 2 + 4

Youngsters build piles of snowballs while reinforcing math skills! Color and cut out an enlarged copy of the snowpal pattern on page 94. Display the snowpal on a background and use a marker to add stick arms. Write a number on a white paper circle (snowball) and attach it to the display. Invite each student to write on a blank snowball a math problem that equals the posted number. Attach each correct snowball to the display. Periodically change the number for more practice.

Use the snowpal cutout again. See page 26.

Winter Words

snowflake

hat

chimney

house

snowman

buttons

tree

door

snow

This simple display encourages reading and writing during the winter season. Have students help you create a winter scene on a board using an enlarged copy of the snowpal pattern on page 94. Attach word cards and a title. Encourage youngsters to read the words and use them when they write.

Use the snowpal cutout again. See page 25.

Student Activities

- **Writing:** Have each student choose three words from the display and incorporate them into a short story.

- **Writing to a prompt:** Ask each student to choose and respond to a prompt such as one of the following:
  Winter is a busy time.
  Making a snowman is so much fun!
  There are lots of things to do when it is cold outside.

- **Describing words:** Have each student copy three words from the display and write two descriptive words for each one.

Sammy

hat   tree
black   big
tall   brown

snow
white
cold

In honor of Hanukkah, have youngsters cook up pretend latkes! Have each child dip a fork in brown paint and make prints that resemble the shredded potato in a latke on a white paper oval. When the paint is dry, have him write his name on his latke. Post an enlarged copy of the mouse chef pattern on page 95 and three plate cutouts labeled as shown. Have each student decide which topping he would prefer and then add his latke to the corresponding plate. Lead youngsters in counting the number of latkes in the resulting stacks to determine the class's favorite topping.

This family art project is sure to get students and their families in a seasonal mood! Copy the tree pattern on page 96 onto white construction paper to make a class supply. Have each student cut out her tree and cover it using squares of various shades of green tissue paper and diluted glue. When her tree has dried, send it home with directions for her family to decorate it to show how they celebrate this time of year. Encourage students to be as creative as possible. When the trees are returned, use them to create a festive display!

Gifts of Great Work

Maya
$5 + 3 = 8$
$3 + 5 = 8$
$8 - 3 = 5$
$8 - 5 = 3$

In the spring, I like to
go to the park.
Jordan

I like to eat scrmld
eggs for brkfst!
Archie

Ethan
$5 + 3 = 8$
$3 + 5 = 8$
$8 - 3 = 5$
$8 - 5 = 3$

Jenny

Flowers smell good.
Roses are my favorite!

Nancy
$5 + 3 = 8$
$3 + 5 = 8$
$8 - 3 = 5$
$8 - 5 = 3$

Students give the gift of great work with these work toppers! Begin by giving each child a copy of a gift box pattern on page 97. Encourage him to color his gift box using crayons or markers. Provide real bows to be added to the tops of the boxes. Ask each student to select a sample of his best work; then display the paper with the matching gift for a display that keeps on giving!

Provide each student with a white paper plate and half of a white paper plate. Instruct her to paint the whole plate with brown tempera paint. From the half plate, have her cut off the rim, paint it to make a collar for the reindeer, and discard the rest. After the paint is dry, instruct her to glue the collar and two hand cutouts (antlers) on the brown plate. Then invite her to add paper ears and a red pom-pom nose. To complete the reindeer, have her draw eyes and a mouth.

Dandy December Reindeer!

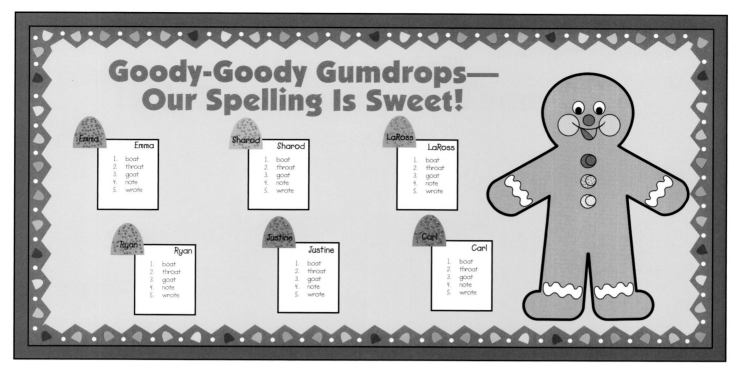

Goody-Goody Gumdrops—
Our Spelling Is Sweet!

Emma
Emma
1. boat
2. throat
3. goat
4. note
5. wrote

Sharod
Sharod
1. boat
2. throat
3. goat
4. note
5. wrote

LaRoss
LaRoss
1. boat
2. throat
3. goat
4. note
5. wrote

Ryan
Ryan
1. boat
2. throat
3. goat
4. note
5. wrote

Justine
Justine
1. boat
2. throat
3. goat
4. note
5. wrote

Carl
Carl
1. boat
2. throat
3. goat
4. note
5. wrote

What better way to spotlight students' sweet success this winter than with gingerbread cookies and gumdrops! Have each child paint a gumdrop cutout with bright-colored paint. Invite him to sprinkle glitter over the wet paint. When the paint is dry, write his name on the gumdrop. When a student shows success or improvement on a spelling test, post his test and gumdrop on a board decorated with an enlarged copy of the gingerbread pal pattern on page 98.

✳ Variations

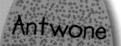

- **Our Work Is Sweet!**
  Display student-chosen work samples with the corresponding gumdrops. Or adjust the title and display exceptional student work in a specific subject area.

- **Aren't We Sweet?**
  Have each child write about what he can do as an act of kindness this holiday season. After he illustrates his work, display his writing with his gumdrop.

- **Gumdrops for Good Behavior**
  Have each child make a gumdrop (without the personalization). When they are dry, place the gumdrops near the board. Each time you observe the class exhibiting positive behaviors, attach a gumdrop to the board. Continue adding gumdrops until all of the gumdrops are displayed. Then reward the class with a special treat.

I can give some of my toys to other kids.

Just as on a traditional Kwanzaa table, where the *muhindi* (ears of corn) represent the number of children in a family, the ears of corn on this display represent the number of youngsters in your classroom family. Post a Kwanzaa table on your board with a *kinara* (candleholder) cutout in the center holding seven paper *mishumaa* (candles). Then have each student glue crumpled pieces of tissue paper onto a corncob cutout (patterns on page 99) for kernels. Display an ear of corn on the table for each child in your class.

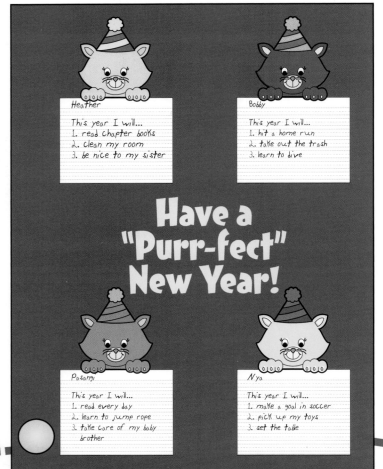

These kittens have their party hats on and are ready to celebrate the New Year by displaying your students' resolutions! On a sheet of writing paper, have each child write "This year I will…" and then list three things he hopes to accomplish in the new year. Have each child color and cut out a copy of the kitten pattern on page 100 and use it as a paper topper to show off his goals for the new year!

Frosty Friends

These snazzy snowpals welcome one and all to winter! Invite each student to follow the directions below to create her own cool character. After it's assembled, encourage her to design and add a face as well as a hat, a scarf, mittens, and any other personal touch. Add the decorated snowpals to a wintry scene for all to enjoy!

Snowpal

Supplies:
three 3" x 12" strips of white construction paper
construction paper scraps of various colors
tape or stapler
glue
markers

Steps:
1. Form each strip into a separate loop and secure each one with tape or staples.
2. Staple or tape the loops together so they resemble a snowpal's body.
3. Glue scraps of paper and use markers to add the face and other details.

Pairs of mittens showcase youngsters' favorite books! Have each child cut out a construction paper copy of the mitten patterns on page 102. Direct her to write the title of a favorite book on one mitten and draw an illustration about the book on the other mitten. Help her use tape to connect the mittens with curling ribbon. Display the completed mittens on a board and watch students cozy up to new books!

Find out about students' winter favorites with a cocoa glyph! Have each child cut out a copy of the mug pattern and glyph key on page 101. Lead students in reading and following the directions on the glyph. Showcase students' mugs and an enlarged copy of the key on a board.

Unique Like Snowflakes

Youngsters' unique qualities glisten with this cool display! After each child makes a lift-the-flap snowflake (see below), ask him to write and illustrate on the blank paper something special about himself. Staple each project to the board so it can be opened.

Lift-the-Flap Snowflake

Supplies:
small student photo
two 8" white construction paper squares
9" blue construction paper square
scissors
glue

Steps:
1. Fold and cut one white paper square into a unique snowflake design.
2. Unfold the snowflake and glue it to the blue paper.
3. Glue the photo to the snowflake's center.
4. Staple the unused white paper behind the blue paper.
5. Trim the edges of the resulting project to match the snowflake's shape.

I can play basketball.
Ethan

Polar Bear, Polar Bear, Are You Here?

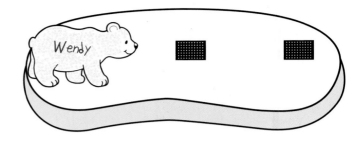

For this attendance display, cut iceberg shapes from white paper and display them near the classroom door. Have each child write his name on a tagboard polar bear cutout (patterns on page 103) and paint it with diluted white paint. Then have him sprinkle glitter over the wet paint. After the paint dries, laminate the cutouts and then attach corresponding Velcro fasteners to the backs of the bears and to the icebergs. Store the bears near the display. Ask students to attach their bears to the icebergs as they arrive each day.

Have each child use art materials to create a penguin. Then ask her to write on a speech bubble cutout a polite phrase that a penguin might say if it could speak. Display each penguin with its speech bubble on a titled board.

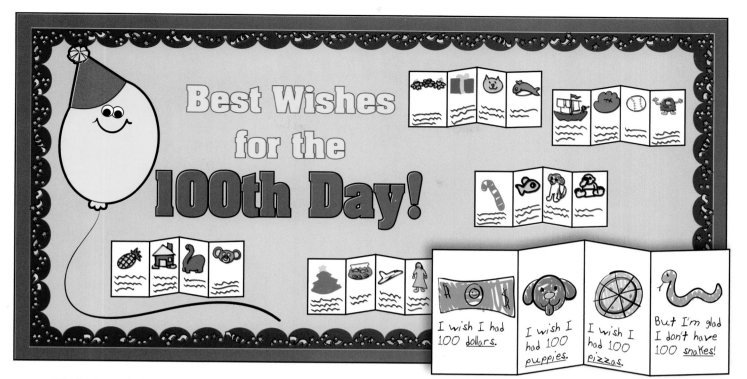

To help celebrate the 100th day of school, give each student a length of paper accordion-folded into fourths. Direct him to program his paper with the sentence starters shown. Then have him complete the sentences and illustrate each section. Color an enlarged copy of the balloon pattern on page 81 and mount it on the board along with your students' wishes for a happy 100th Day display!

Encourage students to talk about the meaning of Valentine's Day with this door display. Make a class supply of heart cutouts and program each one with "Love is…" Give a heart to each child and invite her to complete the sentence. Arrange the hearts on a door or wall for a display with a lot of heart!

Sweets for Sale

Candy Menu

(rolled candy)	= 1¢
(swirl mint)	= 5¢
(heart)	= 10¢
(marshmallow)	= 15¢
(chocolate)	= 25¢

Betsy — 18¢
Chip — 27¢
Earle — 61¢
Elizabeth — 43¢
Wesley — 39¢
Rebecca — 80¢

For a sweet way to give students practice using money, cut out several copies of the candy patterns on page 104 and sort the pieces into separate containers. Post a menu showing the candy choices and their prices. Program a price tag with a different money amount for each student. Give each child a price tag and a construction paper heart. Direct him to "buy" candy equal in cost to the amount on his tag. After you have checked his work, have him color the candy to match the menu and glue it to his heart. Then direct him to add his name and the price tag. Display the resulting candy boxes with the menu to create a priceless Valentine's Day display!

✱ Variations

- **Sweet Fact Families**
  Program each price tag with three numbers that make a fact family. On the heart, a student writes the four number sentences belonging to that fact family and adds candy decorations around them.

- **Adding Treats**
  Each child writes an addition number sentence on his price tag. On his heart, he glues candy that represents that number sentence.

- **Sweet Synonyms**
  Program each price tag with a word that has multiple synonyms. Have each student choose a tag and then write as many synonyms as he can on his heart.

glad
joyful
excited

happy

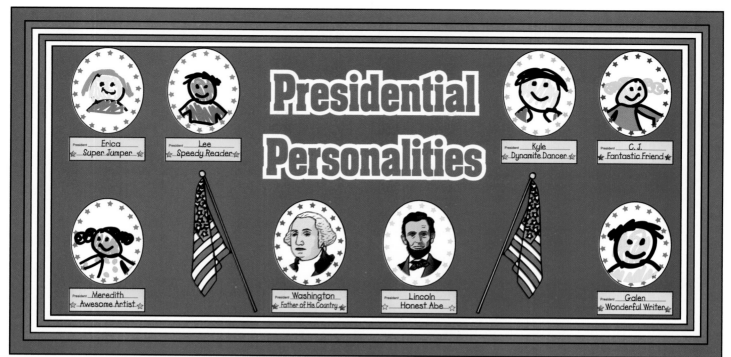

Recognize Presidents' Day by posting pictures of George Washington and Abraham Lincoln. Post their nicknames under the pictures and discuss the character traits that led to these names. Have each student cut out a copy of the frame and nameplate patterns on page 105. Ask her to draw her own portrait inside the frame. On the nameplate, have her write her name after "President" and then have her create a nickname that represents her own personality. Post the portraits and nameplates on the display.

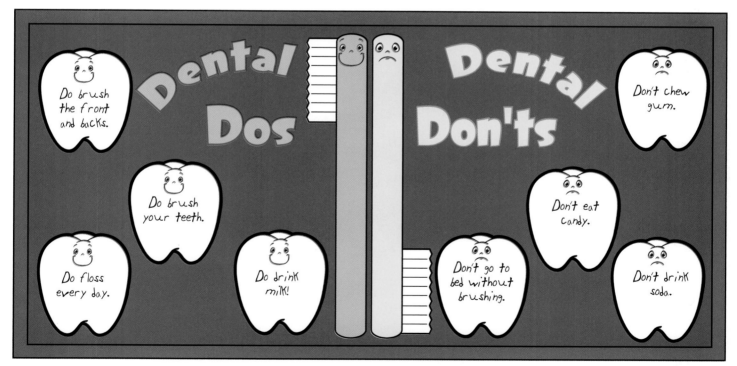

Help your students brush up on good dental health habits! Copy and cut out one of the tooth patterns on page 106 for each child and distribute the teeth. If a student has a smiling tooth, he writes on the tooth something he should do for good dental health. If he has a frowning tooth, he writes something he should avoid doing in order to have good dental health. Divide the board using two oversize toothbrush cutouts and then post the dos on one side and the don'ts on the other.

Wrap up a study of famous African Americans during Black History Month by highlighting facts students have learned. Have each student fold a sheet of white paper in half like a book. After she reopens the paper, direct her to draw on the right half a picture of an African American she has learned about. On the left side, direct her to write why this person is important. Then have her glue the paper inside a folded sheet of brown paper and decorate the front of the brown paper so that it resembles a door. Post each student's door on a board to welcome others to learn about these valuable individuals.

Student Activities

- **Presenting Information:** Students take turns coming up to the board and knocking on one of the doors. The child whose door is chosen then shares information about his famous Black American while pretending to be that person.

- **Questioning:** Have each student, in turn, read what she wrote. Afterward, allow three or four students to ask the presenter questions about her person.

Spring

Windy March weather is sure to inspire students to create their own kites! Post a large cloud face and use white chalk to add wind gusts as shown. Give each child a colorful kite cutout (pattern on page 107) and have him write his name on it. Then have him use various art supplies to decorate the kite and add a length of curling ribbon for a tail. To create a 3-D effect, staple the top and bottom of the kite to the board while allowing the center to bulge outward. For an added touch, leave the kite tails loose and periodically position an electric fan near the board so they blow in the wind.

Celebrate Dr. Seuss's birthday (March 2) with student-created book covers. Invite each child to choose her favorite Dr. Seuss book. On a sheet of paper, have her write the title and draw a picture from that book. Then have her write on a blank card what she likes best about the book. Color and cut out an enlarged copy of the hat pattern on page 108. Display the hat along with students' book covers and writing.

Green is all around during St. Patrick's Day. On a sheet of chart paper, write the following sentence starter: "Have you seen…" Invite each child to complete the question with a green item and then sign his name. Have each youngster create the green item he wrote using various green art materials. Display the green items surrounding the class chart.

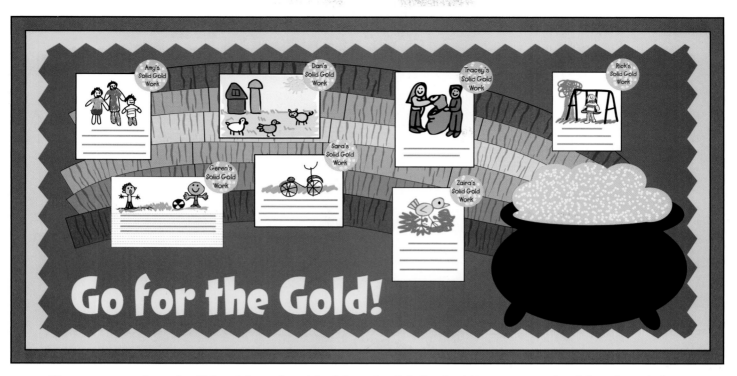

Go for the Gold!

Showcase students' solid gold work with this colorful display! Post a pot of gold and a rainbow made out of streamers or tempera paint. Instruct each student to personalize a coin cutout with her name and the words "Solid Gold Work." Have her spread a thin layer of glue over the coin and sprinkle it with gold glitter. Post a sample of each child's best work on the board with her coin.

Farmer Rabbit's Carrot Patch

This garden is sure to help young-sters' higher-level addition skills grow! Color and cut out an enlarged copy of the rabbit pattern on page 109. Display the rabbit and a basket shape. Cut out a supply of carrots (patterns on page 110). Program a carrot with a number from 10 to 18 and attach it to the rabbit's paw. Ask each student to write on a carrot an addition sentence that uses three addends to equal the posted number. After checking her problem, have her add a green carrot top and help her attach her carrot to the display. Periodically change the posted number for more practice.

Use the rabbit cutout again. See pages 42 and 47.

This seasonal display will inspire students to read and write about everything springlike! Have students help you create a spring scene on a board. Add an enlarged copy of the rabbit pattern on page 109. Attach word cards to label seasonal items. Encourage youngsters to read the words and use them when they write.

Use the rabbit cutout again. See pages 41 and 47.

Student Activities

- **Creative writing:** A student pretends to be the farmer in the display and writes a story about what she will grow in her garden.

- **Writing to a prompt:** A student chooses and responds to a prompt such as one of the following:
  Spring is a time for…
  I would love to plant a garden!
  If I were a bird,…

- **Alphabetical order:** A student writes five words from the board in alphabetical order.

Springtime Symmetry

Make a construction paper copy of the butterfly pattern on page 111 for each student. Have her cut out the butterfly and fold it in half, wing to wing. Instruct her to open the butterfly, drop small amounts of paint onto one wing, and then carefully refold the cutout. After she opens the butterfly and adds pipe cleaner antennae, point out that symmetrical designs were created. Display the colorful creatures on a wall or board.

Shake off the rainy day blues by discussing the positives of a drippy day! Make a class supply of the raindrop pattern on page 112. Instruct each student to write about what he likes to do in the rain or why he likes rain. Have him cut out the raindrop, glue it onto light blue construction paper, and cut it out again, leaving a construction paper border. Post the writing on a door with a colorful umbrella accent at the top.

April Showers!

Olivia
I like to splash in puddles. I have pink rain boots!

Pedro
I like to read inside and listen to the rain on the roof.

Dawn
Rain helps the flowers grow. It makes everything green.

Carol
After it rains, I like to look for rainbows!

Sunjay
After it rains, I like to look for earthworms.

Chip
I like to catch raindrops on my tongue!

How Tall Does Your Garden Grow?

A flower garden provides a perfect way for students to practice measurement skills. Post several flowers with straight stems of varying lengths. Number the flower blossoms from left to right. Have each child write her name on a ladybug cutout (patterns on page 113) and then place it in a designated basket. Remove a ladybug and give that child a measurement direction such as "Place your ladybug six inches up the stem of flower four." The student uses a ruler to measure from the bottom of the stem, writes her measurement on the board, and then tapes her bug in place. Continue in the same manner until each child has had a turn.

✳ Variations

- **Where Will the Ladybug Land?**
  Put the ladybugs in one basket and cards labeled with ordinal number words (that correspond with the flowers) in another basket. Pull a ladybug from the basket and invite that child to draw an ordinal number word, read it, and attach his ladybug to the corresponding flower.

- **Opposites Attract**
  Cut out one ladybug for each flower on the board. Write a word on each ladybug and its antonym on a flower. Have a youngster select a ladybug from a basket and read its word. Then have her locate the antonym for that word and attach the ladybug to the corresponding flower. If desired, laminate the ladybugs before writing the words so that they can be reused with different sets of words.

JUST DUCKY!

For this interactive display, program several duck cutouts (pattern on page 114) with different coin amounts using coin stickers or stamps. Display within students' reach three paper ponds labeled as shown. Attach a strip of blue bulletin board border underneath the ponds. Slide the ducks behind the border and secure them with Sticky-Tac. Invite a student to count the coins on a duck and attach it to the correct pond. After checking her answer, invite a different child to take a turn. Play continues until all ducks have been placed.

Encourage a basketful of good behavior! Cut a large basket out of bulletin board paper, decorate it as desired, and then mount it on a board. Copy and cut out several construction paper chicks (pattern on page 114). On the back of each chick, write a class reward or privilege. Post the chicks and basket on a board. When the class displays good behavior, cooperation, or citizenship, invite a student to pick a chick. Assist him in removing the chick and reading the reward to the class.

...and a _pig_ popped out!

Virginia

...and a _football_ popped out!

Dave

The other day, I gave a shout when an egg cracked open...

...and a _cheeseburger_ popped out!

Bryan

...and a _diamond ring_ popped out!

Donna

...and a _Kitten_ popped out!

Liz

...and a _clown_ popped out!

Jeff

Decorative eggs are the inspiration for this creative-writing project. Present youngsters with the prompt shown on the board. Have each child complete the prompt at the top of a sheet of construction paper by writing "...and a _____ popped out." He fills in the blank with an object of his choice. As an accompaniment to the writing, invite each child to create a colorful sandy egg (see below). After he glues the egg to his paper, have him add a picture of the item popping out. Add the completed projects to the board for an "egg-popping" display!

Sandy Egg

Supplies:
clear Con-Tact paper
colored sand
glitter

Setup:
Trim the Con-Tact paper into an egg shape and remove the backing.

Steps:
1. Sprinkle colored sand and glitter onto the sticky side of the egg.
2. When a desired effect is achieved, shake off the excess sand and glitter.
3. Cut the egg in half using a zigzag pattern.

Assign each student a word family and have her write it in the center of a flower cutout (pattern on page 115). Instruct her to write a word from that word family on each of the petals. After checking the words, invite her to lightly color the flower and glue on a construction paper stem and leaves. "Plant" the flowers on a board along with an enlarged copy of the rabbit pattern on page 109.

Use the rabbit cutout again. See pages 41 and 42.

Hit a home run with this motivational display! Mount a baseball diamond on the wall. In the center of the diamond, post a goal that you would like the class to work on, such as being quiet during work time or cleaning up after centers. Color and cut out a copy of the baseball buddy pattern on page 115 and use Sticky-Tac to attach it next to home plate. Each time you observe the class displaying the goal behavior, move the buddy to the next base. When a run is scored, reward the class and then post a new goal.

Display your youngsters'"bee-utiful" work with these busy bees! Mount an enlarged copy of the beehive pattern on page 140 in the center of a board. Have each student cut out and personalize a yellow construction paper copy of a bee pattern on page 116. Post each child's bee with a chosen work sample.

* Variations

- **We're Buzzing About Facts and Opinions!**
  Post two large beehives on a board. Label one "Fact" and the other "Opinion." Program each of a supply of bee cutouts with a different fact or opinion statement. Label the backs for self-checking. Use Sticky-Tac to post the bees around the hives. When a student visits the board, he sorts the bees onto the correct hives.

- **We're Buzzing About Punctuation!**
  Program the backs of a class supply of bee cutouts with different ending punctuation marks. Give each student a bee and have her write a sentence on the front of her bee that uses the given punctuation mark. Post three large beehive cutouts labeled with different ending punctuation marks. Attach the bees to the matching hives.

Bees are yellow and black.

Students are sure to sparkle with pride as they write about their mothers! Begin by making a class supply of construction paper jewels (patterns on page 117). Invite each youngster to select a jewel and write about his mother or another special woman in his life on a same-size sheet of blank paper. Help him staple his jewel atop his writing so that the project can be opened. Invite each child to decorate his jewel; then post the completed projects on a board.

On a wall, post a large paper jam jar. Copy and cut out several red paper strawberries (patterns on page 118). Write a word on each strawberry so that you have several pairs of synonyms. Place the strawberries in a basket near the display. When a child visits the jam jar, she spreads out the strawberries and pairs up the words that have the same meaning. She then attaches them to the jar cutout using Sticky-Tac.

Ms. Chapman's Sweet Treats!

Get youngsters in the mood for summer with this sweet art activity! Invite students to make fruity gelatin-paint ice pops (see below). Post the sweet-smelling treats for a cool display!

Fruity Gelatin-Paint Ice Pops

Supplies:

white construction paper ice pop
   cutouts (pattern on page 118)
large package of sugar-free gelatin
   in each of the following flavors:
   orange, cherry, grape, and lime
boiling water (for teacher use only)

cold water
small plastic bowls
wooden craft sticks
paintbrushes
clear or white glitter
diluted glue

Setup:

Empty each box of gelatin into a separate bowl. Add slightly less than one-fourth cup of boiling water to each bowl. Stir the mixture until the powder is dissolved. Add enough cold water to total one-fourth cup of water. Allow paint to cool before giving to students. Use the paints within 30 minutes so that the gelatin doesn't set.

Steps:

1. Select a flavor of gelatin paint and use it to paint the ice pop cutout.
2. After the paint dries, brush diluted glue over the ice pop and sprinkle on glitter.
3. Write your name on a craft stick and glue it to your ice pop.

End of the Year

We're Ready...

To Take a Bite out of Summer!

Count down the final days of school with this cool watermelon slice! Use bulletin board paper to make a large watermelon slice with a bite taken out of it; then post it on the wall. For each remaining day of school, cut out a black paper watermelon seed. Number the seeds and attach them to the slice. Each day, invite a child to flip over the next seed to show how many days remain in the school year.

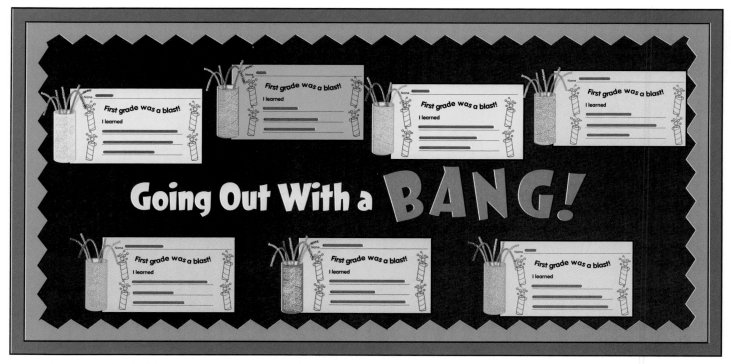

Have each child write on a copy of the recording sheet on page 119 three things she has learned during first grade. Then have her make a firecracker craft (see below). Mount each child's completed craft and recording sheet on the board. Students will burst with pride as they remember their accomplishments!

Firecracker

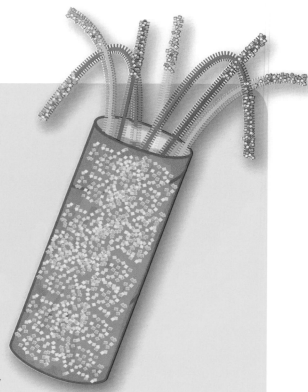

Supplies:
small cardboard tube
pipe cleaners cut into half lengths
colorful paints
paintbrush
glitter
markers
tape

Steps:
1. Use the paints to decorate the tube.
2. When the tube is dry, use markers and glitter to add details.
3. Add glitter to the end of each pipe cleaner by rolling it in glue and then in glitter.
4. Tape the dried pipe cleaners to the inside edge of the firecracker and bend them outward to show the explosion.

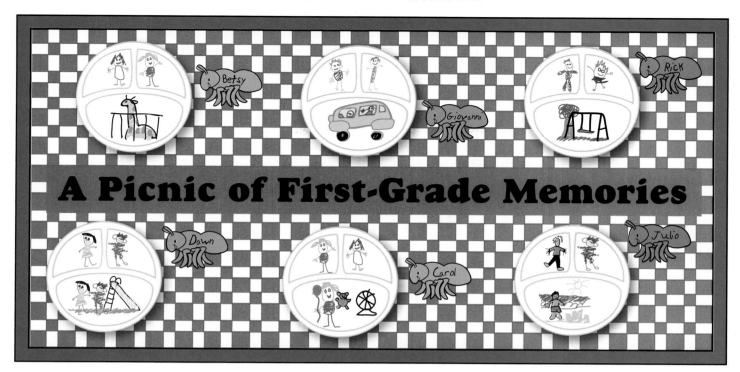

Serve up first-grade memories with this fantastic board! Provide each student with a paper plate with three sections. Encourage her to recall the year by drawing herself in one section, a friend in another section, and a favorite field trip or class activity in the remaining section. Have each child write her name on an ant cutout (pattern on page 119). Display the ants with the plates on a board covered with a checkered tablecloth.

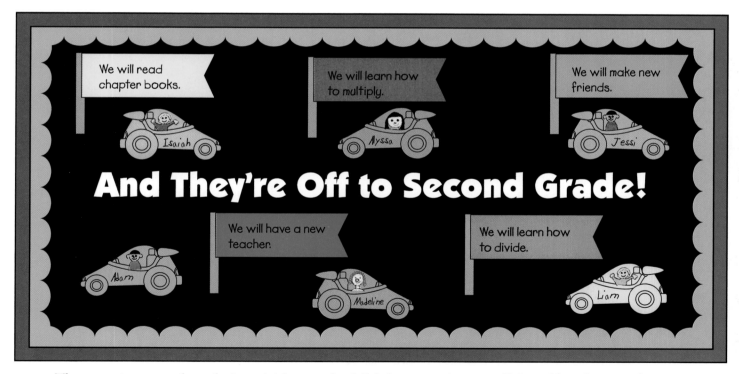

The race to second grade is on! After each child draws a picture of himself and writes his name on a racecar cutout (patterns on page 120), mount the cars on the board. To complete the display, enlist students' help in listing things they look forward to in second grade. Write each idea on a colorful flag and scatter the flags around the cars on the board.

Brighten up the classroom and get youngsters ready for summer fun! On an orange or yellow construction paper triangle (ray), have each child write something she plans to do during summer vacation. Arrange the rays around a construction paper copy of the smiling sun pattern on page 121 and watch the summer excitement heat up!

This eye-catching door display will help launch your students into second grade! Cover a door with black paper and, if desired, add star, planet, and comet cutouts. Have each student cut out a copy of the rocket pattern on page 122 and write what he looks forward to learning in second grade. After each student adds a photo of himself to the window, have him tape shiny curled lengths of ribbon to the rocket. Mount the rockets on the door for a display that's out of sight!

Away We Go!

Help students get moving toward summer with this creative-writing idea. Cut out multiple copies of the vehicle patterns on page 123. Invite each youngster to select one of the vehicles and think about an imaginary summer adventure that he could take while riding in or on that vehicle. Then have him write his idea on paper and decorate his vehicle. Post students' writings and vehicles on a board showing land, water, and air.

 Variations

- **On-the-Go Graphing:**
  Turn the board into a graph and use the vehicle cutouts as graphing pieces. Have students make a graph to show their favorite vehicles or which vehicles they would most like to travel in.

- **Vehicle Vocabulary:**
  During a study of transportation, use the patterns on page 123 as well as additional vehicle cutouts—such as a motorcycle, bicycle, bus, and train—to create a transportation scene. Label each vehicle with its name and encourage youngsters to use the board as a reference throughout your transportation study.

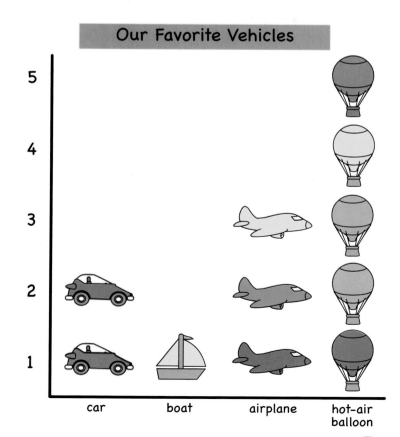

Our Favorite Vehicles

Stir up sweet memories and prepare next year's students for the year ahead with this writing activity. Copy the writing pattern on page 124 onto yellow paper to make a class supply. Give each child a pattern and encourage her to complete each sentence. Have her slip the completed pattern into a clear plastic cup and top it off with a fun straw. Use pushpins to attach the cups to a board and add a paper lemonade stand. Start the next year by reading these cool favorites to a new class!

Highlight students' spectacular work with this festive display. Have each child color and cut out a construction paper copy of the paper topper pattern on page 124. If desired, have him add glitter details. Use the toppers to adorn student work for Flag Day, the Fourth of July, or another patriotic occasion.

Anytime

Program each of several monkey cutouts (pattern on page 125) with a different word family; then post the monkeys on a board. Enlist students' help in compiling a list of words for each word family. Write each word on a separate banana cutout (pattern on page 125) and place the bananas near the display. Invite students to feed the monkeys by using Sticky-Tac to attach the bananas below the corresponding monkeys.

Our Writing Tree

Use this idea and the variations below for a yearlong writing prompt display! Post a large tree cutout within students' reach. Program a class supply of leaf cutouts (pattern on page 88) with writing prompts. Arrange the leaves on the tree with Sticky-Tac or Velcro fasteners for easy movement. To use the tree, have each youngster remove a leaf and respond to the prompt in his journal. After he completes his entry, have him return the leaf to the tree.

✳ Variations

- **Fall Into Writing**
  Write new prompts on colorful leaves for the fall months.

- **Winter Writing**
  Write new prompts on snowflake cutouts (pattern on page 88) for the winter months.

- **Writing in Bloom**
  Write new prompts on flower cutouts (pattern on page 88) for the spring months.

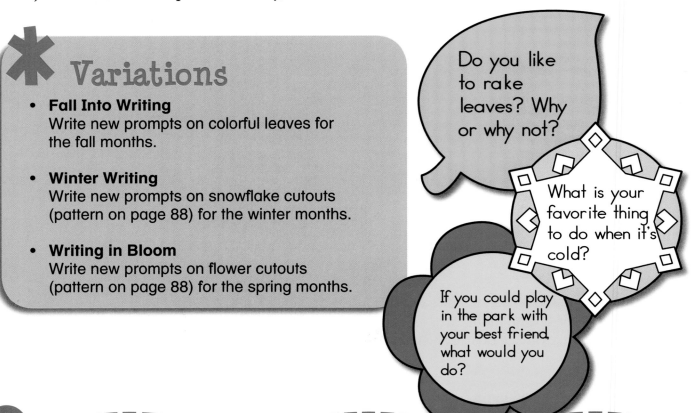

Do you like to rake leaves? Why or why not?

What is your favorite thing to do when it's cold?

If you could play in the park with your best friend, what would you do?

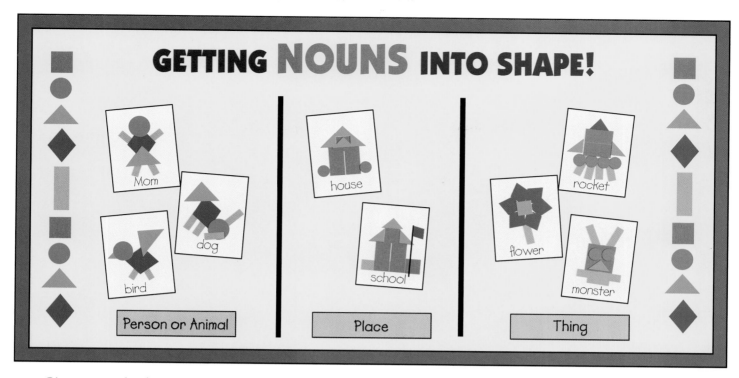

GETTING NOUNS INTO SHAPE!

Person or Animal | Place | Thing

Give a new look to noun classification with this geometric idea! Display cards labeled with the different types of nouns as shown. Have each child glue small shape cutouts to a sheet of construction paper to form a person, animal, place, or thing. After she labels her picture, attach it to the corresponding section of the board to create a noun reference.

A display of friendly letters is sure to boost youngsters' self esteem! Have each child personalize the front of an envelope and draw a stamp. Collect the envelopes and then redistribute them so that each child receives an envelope that is not his own. Then ask each youngster to write a friendly letter to the named person, complimenting him on something he does well. Post the completed letters, envelopes, and an enlarged copy of the mailbox pattern on page 126. (Add a paper post to the mailbox.) Invite students to the board to read the letters.

Our Picture Dictionary

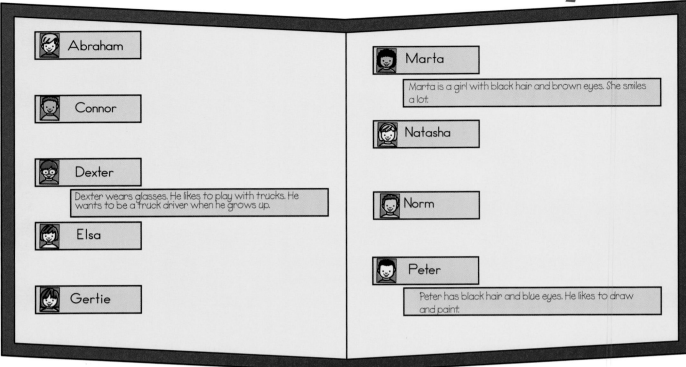

Showcase the students in your classroom with an extra-large picture dictionary! Glue a photo of each youngster to a paper strip labeled with his name. Mount the strips on a book shape so that it resembles a picture dictionary. Then assign each child a different student and have him write on another strip an entry that describes his classmate. Next, read an entry, omitting the name, and help youngsters determine who is described. As your sleuths solve each one, post it by the corresponding student name and photo.

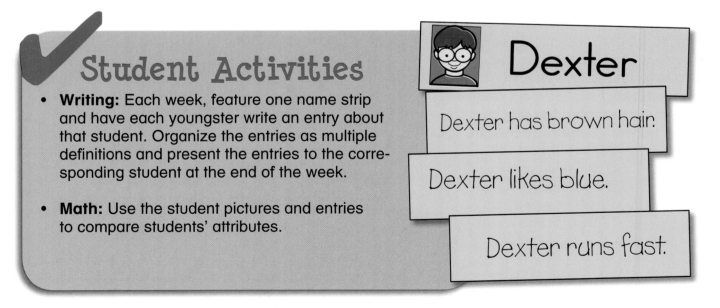

Student Activities

- **Writing:** Each week, feature one name strip and have each youngster write an entry about that student. Organize the entries as multiple definitions and present the entries to the corresponding student at the end of the week.

- **Math:** Use the student pictures and entries to compare students' attributes.

Have each youngster color and cut out a copy of the horse pattern on page 127. Then have her pretend that her horse has gone on an adventure. Instruct her to write on a speech bubble cutout what the horse might say about its adventure. Post each horse and the corresponding speech bubble for a creative-writing display.

This wall display beats traditional skip-counting hands down! Help half your youngsters make prints with their left hands and the other half make prints with their right hands. Alternating between left and right, number the prints in increments of five and then laminate them. Arrange the prints in order within student reach. Finally, have youngsters gently place alternating hands on the numbered prints as they practice counting by fives.

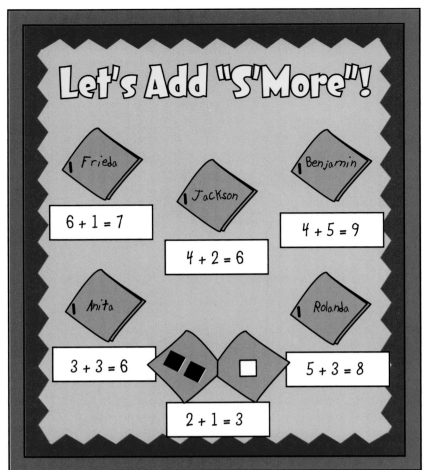

This sweet favorite combines math and art. Help each child make a s'more craft (see below). Have each youngster roll a die, open his s'more, and glue that number of chocolate cutouts to the left side. Then have him roll again and glue that number of marshmallow cutouts to the right side. Direct each youngster to write on a blank card a matching number sentence. Post the s'mores on a board and place the cards nearby. Invite students to match the cards to the s'mores and then mount them on the board.

S'more Craft

Supplies:
flour
2 tagboard squares
paintbrush
brown paint
stapler

Setup:
Mix flour with the light brown paint until a textured consistency is observed.

Steps:
1. Paint both sides of each tagboard square with the brown paint mixture. Let the paint dry.
2. Staple the squares together in the corner.

Elephant Express

4 + 2 =

7 – 1 =

2 + 3 =

2 + 2 =

6 – 3 =

To prepare this interactive addition and subtraction display, cut out and laminate five copies of the train car pattern on page 129. Also cut out a large supply of tagboard copies of the elephant strips on page 128. Use a wipe-off marker to program each car with a different addition or subtraction problem. Then staple both sides and the bottom of each car to the board to form pockets. Invite youngsters to slide the correct number of elephants into each car to show the answer for each problem. For extra practice, simply wipe off the cars and write new math problems.

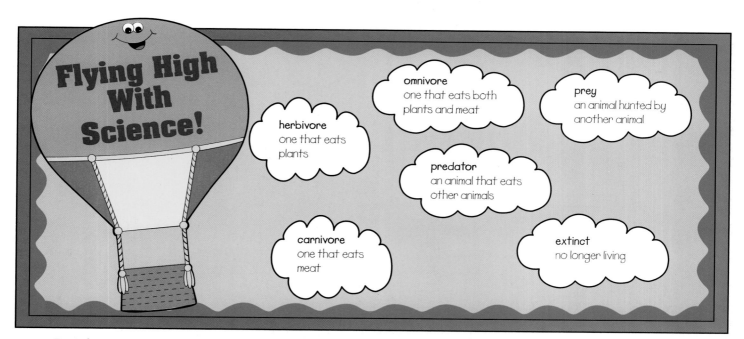

Flying High With Science!

omnivore
one that eats both
plants and meat

prey
an animal hunted by
another animal

herbivore
one that eats
plants

predator
an animal that eats
other animals

carnivore
one that eats
meat

extinct
no longer living

Reinforce science vocabulary with a reusable display! Laminate several cloud cutouts and mount them on a board with an enlarged copy of the hot-air balloon pattern on page 83. Label each cloud with a different science term. Invite students to dictate a definition for each posted word. Then use a wipe-off marker to write the student-generated definitions. As youngsters learn new words, add more clouds or wipe off the displayed ones and use them again!

Are You Through?

Pick a piece for more to do!

Write an entry in our weather log.

Write a letter to a friend.

Write in your journal about something you saw on the way to school.

Read a big book.

If you could have a new pet, what would it be? Answer the question and illustrate your answer.

Create a class graph that shows the kinds of shoes classmates are wearing.

Read a book from your book box.

Use blocks to measure classroom objects. Label your work.

With this display, students will not be puzzled about what to do when they finish their work early! First, brainstorm with youngsters different activities they can do when they finish their work. Then have each youngster write a different activity on a puzzle piece cutout (pattern on page 130). Next, use Velcro fasteners to assemble the puzzle on a wall with a title. When a youngster has extra time after completing a task, invite him to select a puzzle piece, read and do the activity, and return the piece to the wall.

Create a shiny background on your board with wrapping paper of your choice. Have each child personalize and decorate a star cutout (patterns on page 131). Post the completed stars with the corresponding students' finest work. Periodically update the work samples to keep the display shining bright!

Show off each student's best work while collecting pages for a year-end memory book! Program a 12-inch square for each student with his name and grade level. Then have him draw designs around the perimeter of his square. Arrange the completed squares and a title on a bulletin board. If desired, use a marker to draw stitches around the squares. Throughout the year, post each student's favorite or best work atop his square. After changing a work sample, store the old work sample in a file. At the end of the year, make a memory book for each child by binding his filed papers behind his quilt square.

Student Activities

- **Making observations:** Choose for each student two work samples from different times of the year. Have her compare the two pieces and write about her observations.

- **Writing to a prompt:** Have each youngster respond to a writing prompt at the beginning of each season. Use the resulting pages as dividers in each youngster's memory book at the end of the year.

- **Writing:** Select one example of outstanding work displayed on the board. Have each youngster write about what she likes about the featured assignment. Collect the completed pages for a special section of the featured student's work in her memory book. Continue in this manner throughout the year, giving each child a chance to be the star performer.

Use these artsy renditions of your youngsters to quickly rotate outstanding work! After each child makes a personalized bag (see below), place a selected piece of work in each youngster's bag and arrange the completed projects on a board. Then showcase different examples of excellence for each student by simply sliding out the old page and dropping in a new one!

Personalized Bag

Supplies:
copy of the arm and leg patterns on page 132
gallon-size resealable plastic bag
8" construction paper circle
markers
craft materials for facial details
glue
stapler

Steps:
1. Color and cut out the arm and leg patterns.
2. Glue the arms and legs to the bag.
3. Decorate the circle using craft materials and markers so that it resembles your head.
4. Slip the bottom of the head into the top of the bag and staple it to the back.

Call attention to great work with this revved-up display! Secure a green cloth or paper flag to the corner of a bulletin board with a checkered border. Then have each child personalize a racecar cutout (patterns on page 120). Explain to students that when they "start their engines," they are able to produce great work. When a student exemplifies this concept, post her paper and racecar on the display.

Help each youngster select a page of completed work to showcase. Then have him color and cut out a copy of the pirate patterns on pages 133 and 134. Instruct him to glue the cutouts to the top and bottom of his work. Arrange the pirates and a paper treasure chest on a wall to show off your first graders' treasured work!

Taking the Time to Do Our Best Work!

Encourage students to take time to do their best work with this positive display! Color and cut out a copy of the snail pattern on page 135. Then create a snail trail of excellence by posting student work that was completed with a little bit of extra effort!

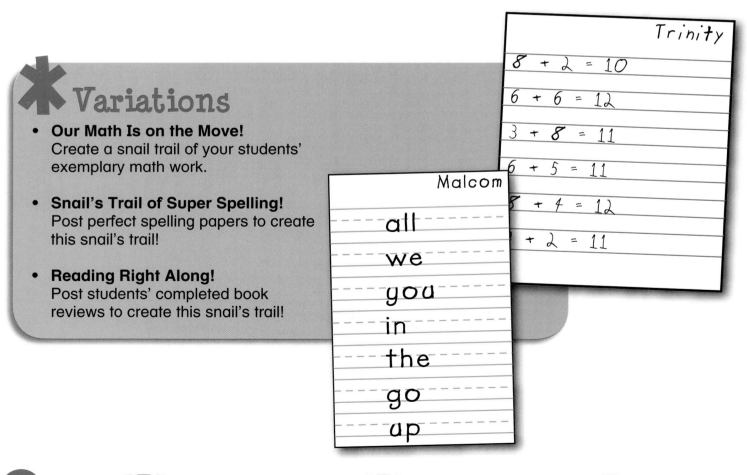

Variations

- **Our Math Is on the Move!**
  Create a snail trail of your students' exemplary math work.

- **Snail's Trail of Super Spelling!**
  Post perfect spelling papers to create this snail's trail!

- **Reading Right Along!**
  Post students' completed book reviews to create this snail's trail!

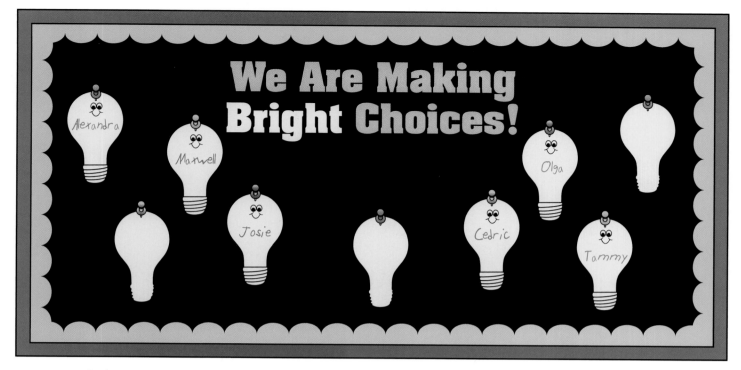

We Are Making Bright Choices!

Spotlight students' good behavior with this bright display! Have each youngster write her name on a lightbulb cutout (patterns on page 136). Use pushpins to attach the lightbulbs to a board. If a youngster's choice does not follow your classroom plan, simply turn her lightbulb around to show that her light has "dimmed" until good choices are demonstrated.

Have each youngster personalize and cut out a copy of a fish pattern on page 137. Arrange the fish on a board and staple three sides of a bucket cutout to the board to create a pocket. If a youngster strays from good behavior, slide his fish into the pocket. Students are sure to do their best to avoid becoming a fish out of water!

Swimming With Good Behavior

Collecting coins in these piggy banks is sure to promote positive behavior! Staple each completed piggy bank (see below) on a board so that the bag is open. When a student demonstrates a positive behavior, write the action on a construction paper circle (coin) and drop it into the piggy bank. Then reward individual students with a certificate or a small treat when a desired number of coins have been earned.

Piggy Bank

Supplies:

copy of the pig patterns on page 138	crayons
white paper lunch bag	marker
half of a pink pipe cleaner	glue
pink paint	pencil
paintbrush	tape

Steps:

1. Paint the bag pink. Let the paint dry.
2. Color, cut out, and glue the patterns to the front of the bag.
3. Wrap the pipe cleaner around a pencil, remove it from the pencil, and then tape it to one side of the bag for a tail.
4. Write your name on the piggy bank.

Simply move these racecars around the track to change classroom jobs. Cut bulletin board paper so it resembles a racetrack. Write each classroom job on a paper flag and post the flags around the track. Then have each student personalize and cut out a copy of each of the racecar patterns on page 120. Place students' cars that face the proper direction around the track to assign jobs. As each rightward-facing car crosses the halfway point around the track, exchange it for the leftward-facing car with the same student's name. When a car reaches the finish line, remove that car and move a new car to the starting line to begin another student's trip of responsibilities!

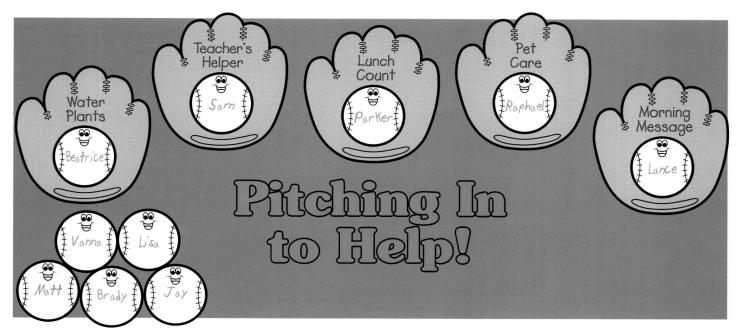

These baseball mitts are just perfect for catching helpers! Have each student write his name on a baseball cutout (patterns on page 139). Write job names on individual mitt cutouts (pattern on page 139) and attach them to a wall. Then assign student responsibilities by using Sticky-Tac to attach a baseball to each mitt. Stack the remaining baseballs nearby to quickly change jobs as desired.

To ensure that students, parents, and other teachers know what skills you are working on, use this buzz board! Write a different skill or topic on each of several beehive cutouts (pattern on page 140). Have each youngster personalize a bee cutout (patterns on page 116). Each week, display the student bees and the appropriate hives. Classroom visitors are sure to stop and check out what your busy bees are learning!

Welcome youngsters each morning with this attendance display! For each student, cut a tagboard oval in half so it resembles a cracked egg and fasten the halves with a brad. Have each youngster write her name on her egg and then color and cut out a copy of a chick pattern on page 114. Help her glue her chick to the egg so that when the egg is opened, her chick is peeking out. Staple the bottom half of each egg to a board. Finally, invite each youngster to crack open her egg each morning to announce her arrival.

Announce the daily lunch menu with this display! Brainstorm with youngsters different food choices prepared in the cafeteria. Write student responses on individual cards and give each child a card to illustrate. Post the cards, a large paper lunch tray, and an enlarged copy of the spoon patttern on page 141 on a board. Each morning, review the day's menu and move the corresponding cards to the tray, making additional cards when necessary.

Student Activities

- **Writing:** Give each youngster one food card. Have him write about whether he likes the food pictured.

- **Math:** Invite students to sort the cards that aren't on the tray by different attributes. Encourage them to think of new attributes each day.

- **Science and health:** Use the board to discuss balanced meals as described by the USDA Food Guide Pyramid. Then have youngsters draw an appetizing balanced meal.

I don't like to eat spaghetti. It's too messy.

Rocket and Planet Patterns
Use with "First Grade Is a Blast!" on page 5.

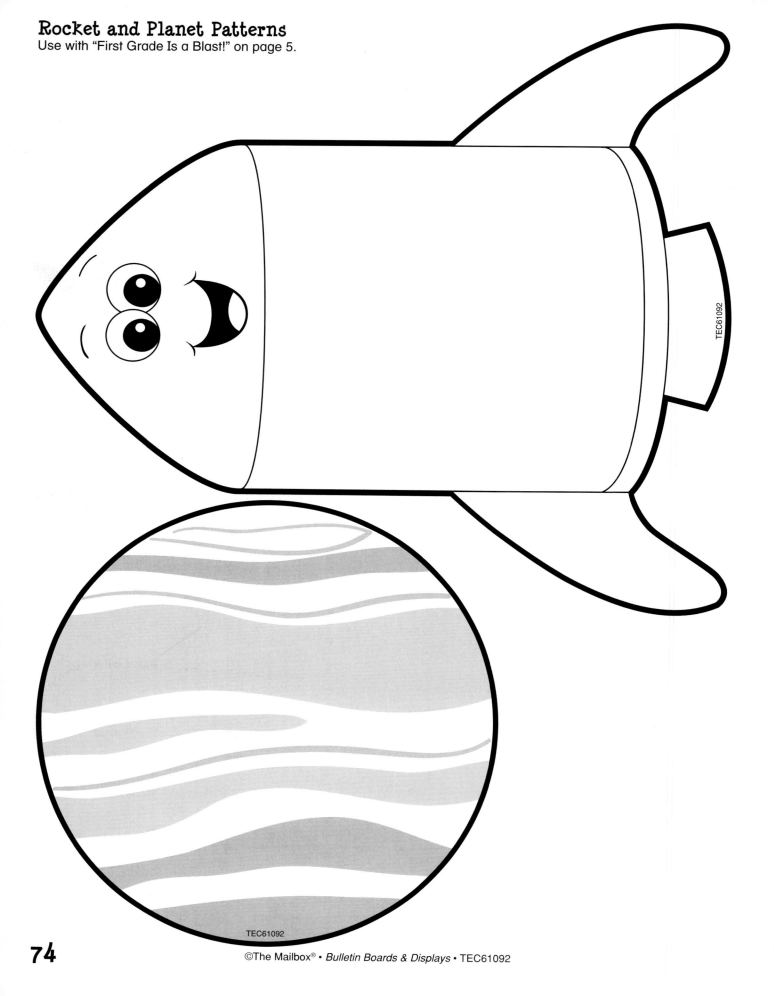

TEC61092

Pencil Pattern
Use with "First Grade Is 'Write' On!" on page 8.

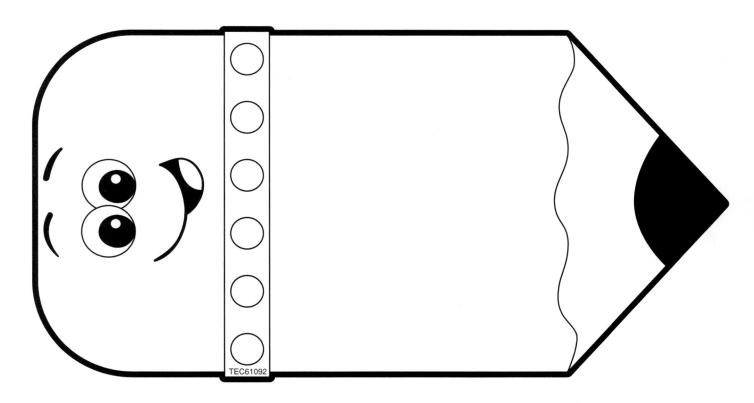

TEC61092

Magnifying Glass Pattern
Use with "Where in the World Have You Been?" on page 12.

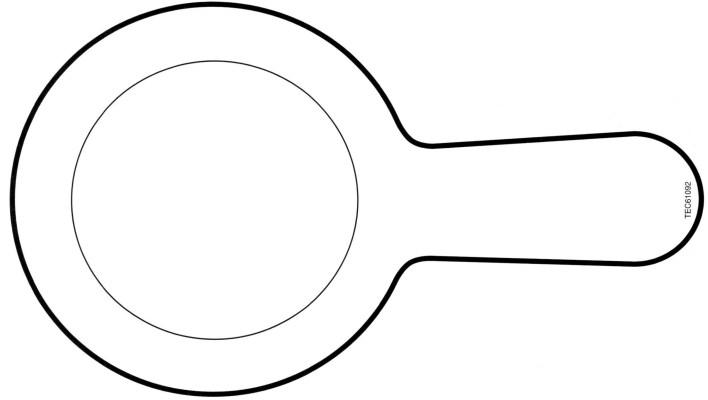

TEC61092

Owl Pattern

Use with "'Whoooo's' in Ms. Lumley's Class?" on page 9, "Who Am I?" on page 11, and "'Whoooo' Likes Which Pie?" on page 24.

TEC61092

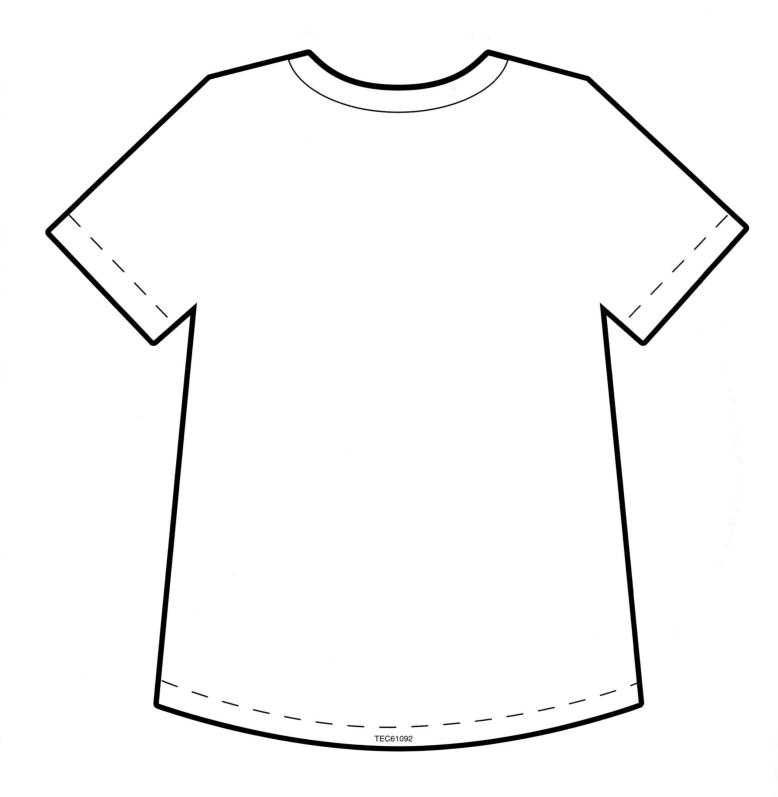

TEC61092

Person Patterns
Use with "I Am Here Today" on page 11.

TEC61092

TEC61092

bus

bike

walk

car

TEC61092

TEC61092

TEC61092

TEC61092

Globe Character Pattern

Use with "Where in the World Have You Been?" on page 12.

TEC61092

TEC61092

Ferris Wheel Seat Patterns
Use with "Wheel of Helpers" on page 13.

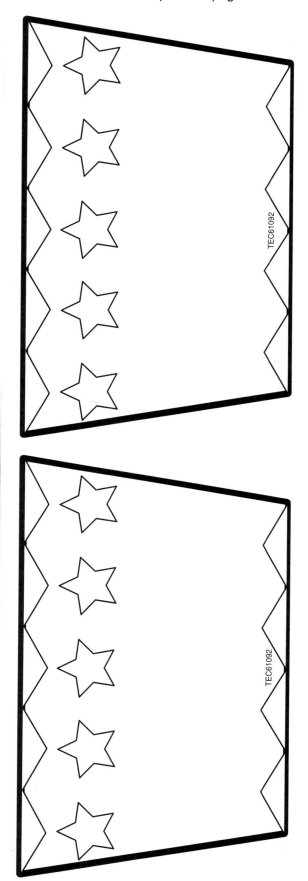

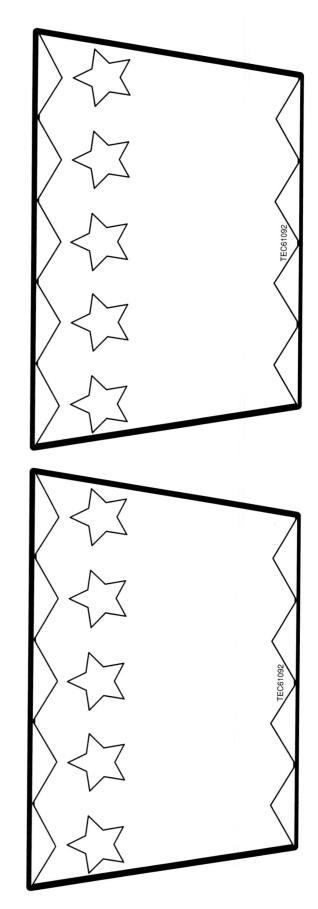

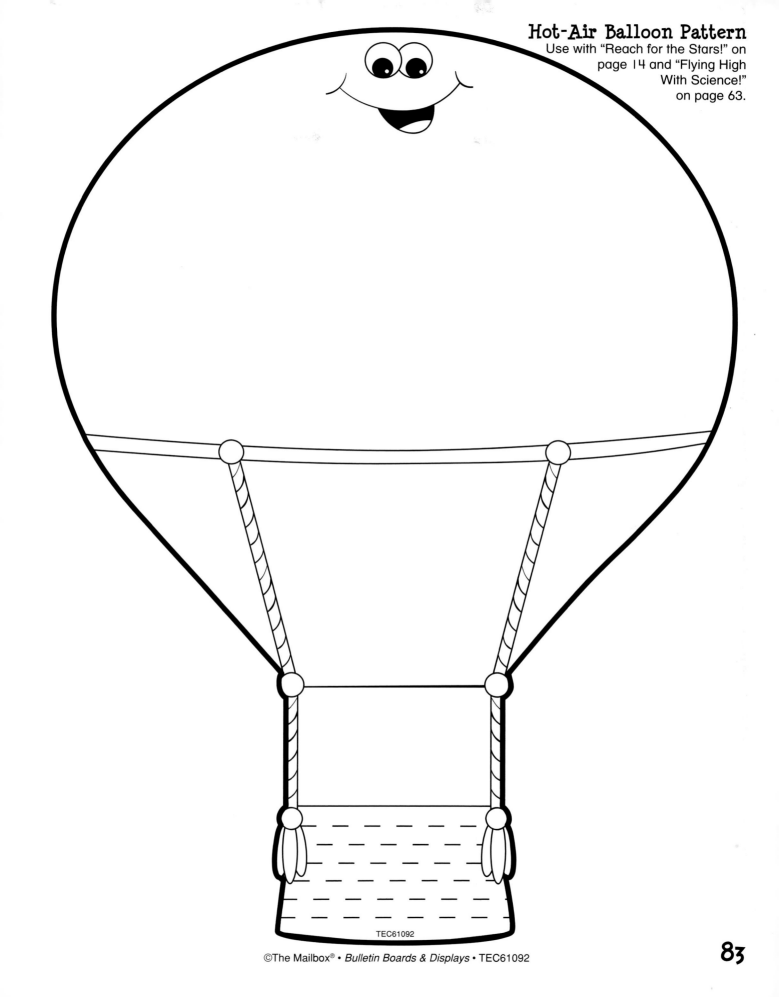

Hot-Air Balloon Pattern
Use with "Reach for the Stars!" on page 14 and "Flying High With Science!" on page 63.

TEC61092

Apple Pattern
Use with "A Descriptive Harvest" on page 15.

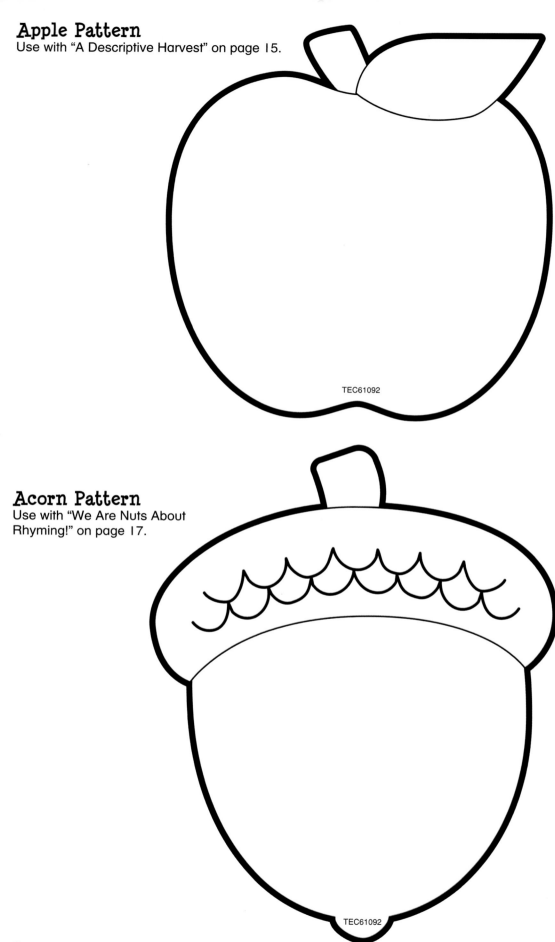

TEC61092

Acorn Pattern
Use with "We Are Nuts About Rhyming!" on page 17.

TEC61092

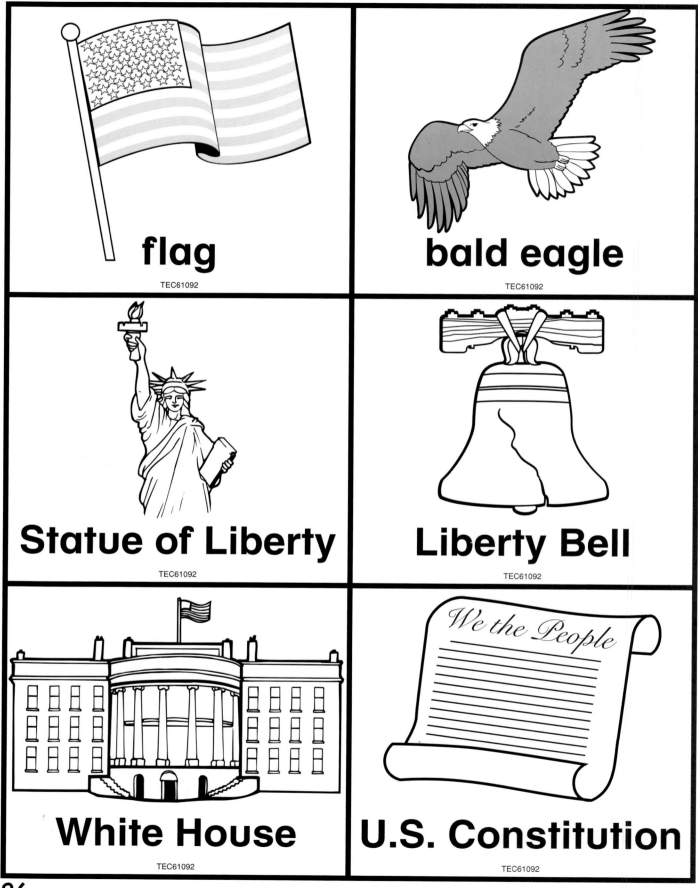

flag

bald eagle

Statue of Liberty

Liberty Bell

White House

U.S. Constitution

TEC61092

We the People

TEC61092

Leaf, Snowflake, and Flower Patterns
Use with "Fall Is 'Grrrr-eat'!" on page 18 and "Our Writing Tree" on page 58.

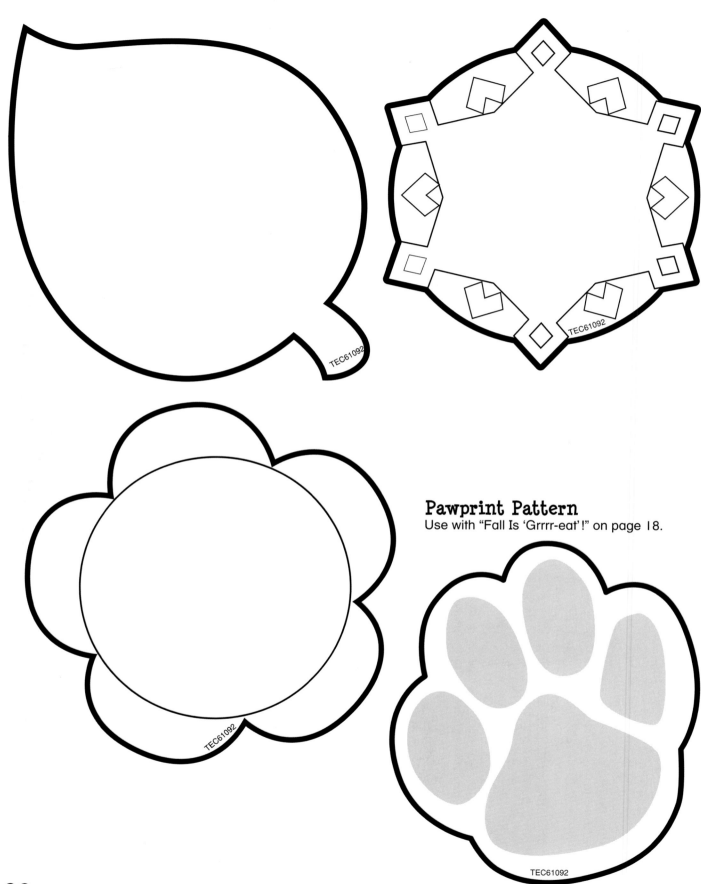

TEC61092

TEC61092

Pawprint Pattern
Use with "Fall Is 'Grrrr-eat'!" on page 18.

TEC61092

TEC61092

Spider Cards
Use with "Webs of Measurements" on page 20.

©The Mailbox® • *Bulletin Boards & Displays* • TEC61092

Title: _____

Author: _____

Student name: _____

Glue.

I liked it when_____

_____

_____

Glue.

TEC61092

Scarecrow Clothes Patterns
Use with "Scarecrow Math" on page 21.

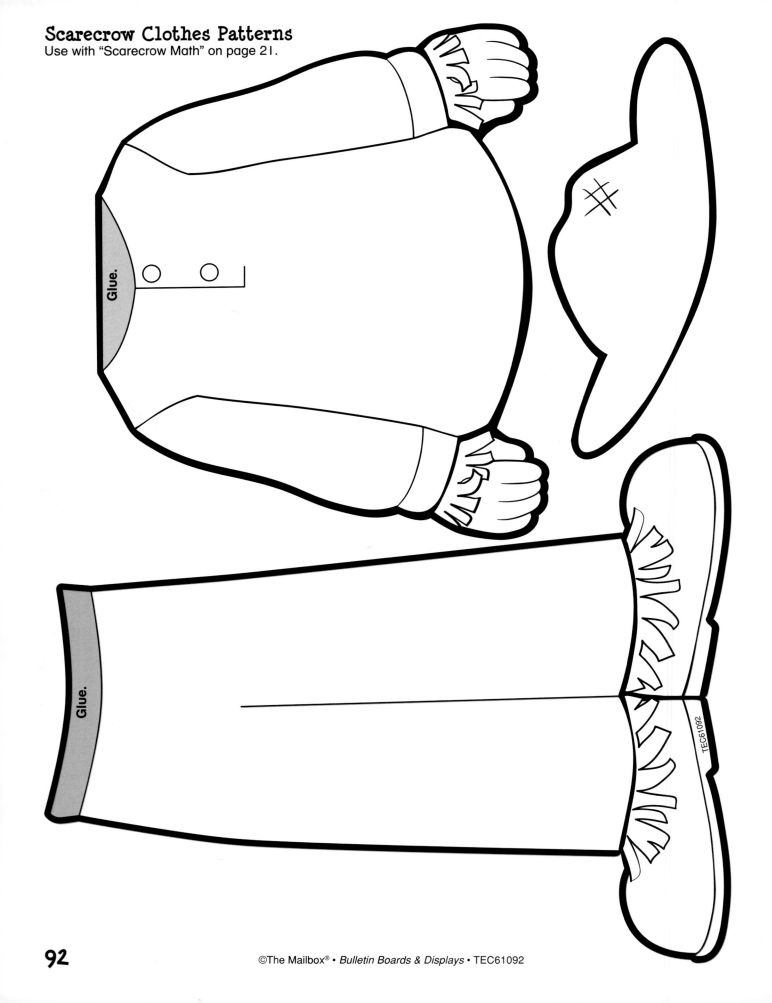

Glue.

Glue.

TEC61092

Car Pattern
Use with "Reading Road" on page 22.

TEC61092

Turkey Pattern
Use with "We Are Thankful" on page 23.

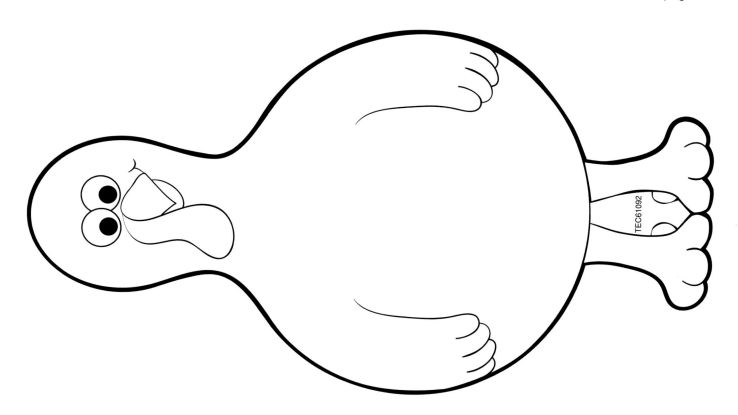

TEC61092

Snowpal Pattern

Use with "Snowball Math" on page 25
and "Winter Words" on page 26.

TEC61092

Tree Pattern
Use with "Trees of the Season" on page 27.

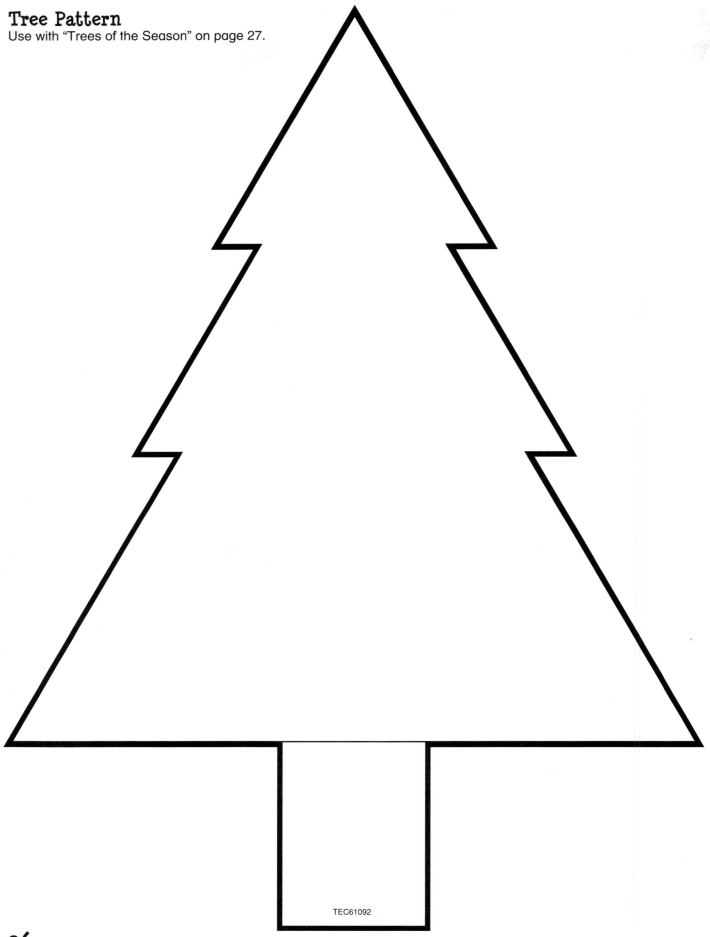

TEC61092

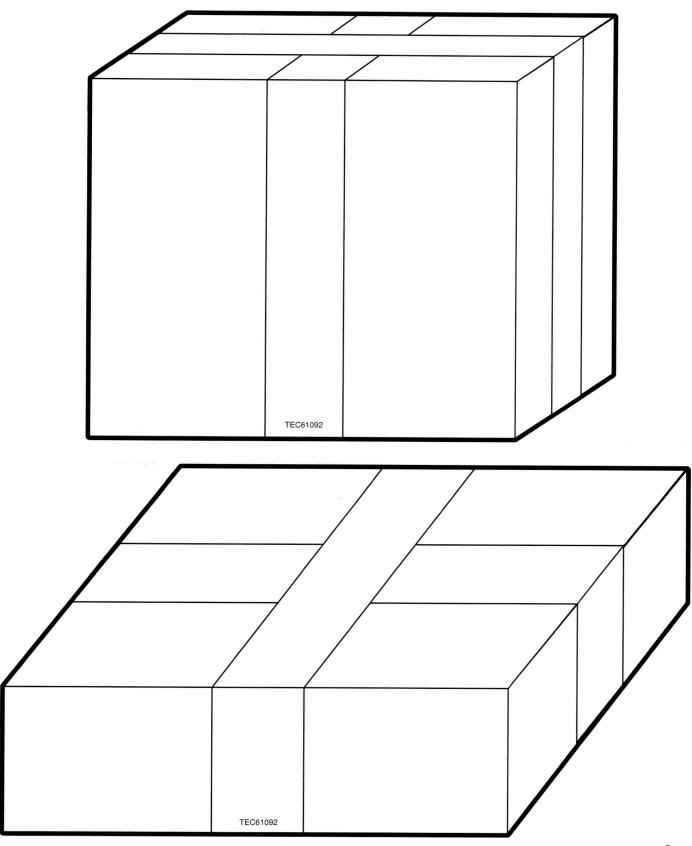

TEC61092

TEC61092

Gingerbread Pal Pattern

Use with "Goody-Goody Gumdrops—
Our Spelling Is Sweet!" on page 29.

TEC61092

Use with "Habari Gani! Welcome to Our Kwanzaa Table!" on page 30.

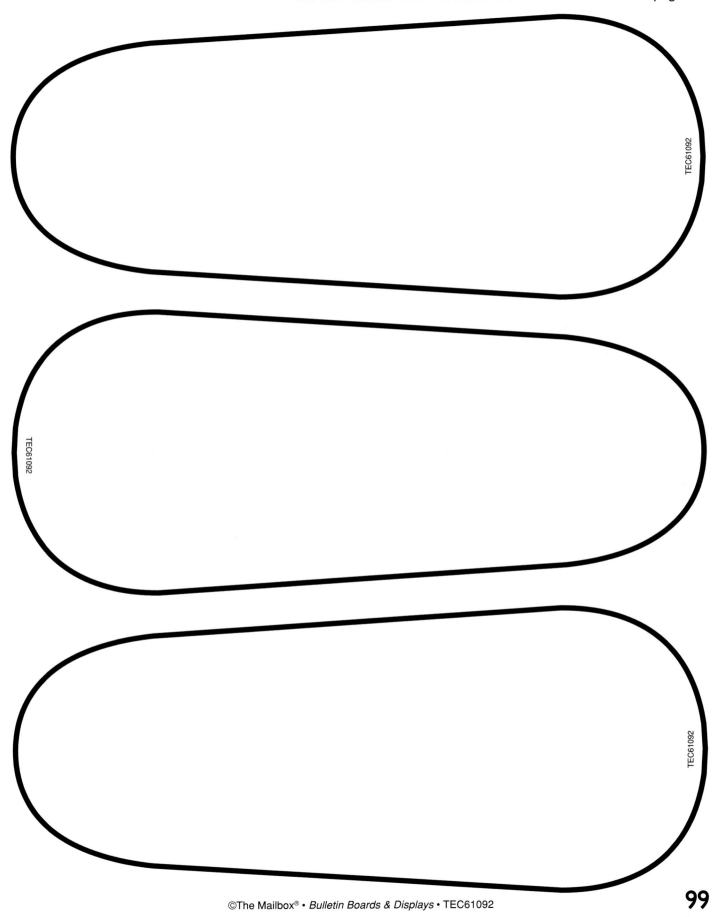

TEC61092

TEC61092

TEC61092

Kitten Pattern
Use with "Have a 'Purr-fect' New Year!" on page 30.

TEC61092

100

Winter Favorites Glyph Key

Have you ever played in the snow?

Yes—Color the hat black.

No—Color the hat orange.

Do you like cold weather?

Yes—Draw four buttons on the snowpal.

No—Draw two buttons on the snowpal.

What is your favorite winter activity?

Sledding—Color your mug red.

Baking cookies—Color your mug green.

Playing inside—Color your mug yellow.

Other—Color your mug blue.

Do you like to drink hot cocoa?

Yes—Glue on 4 paper marshmallows.

No—Glue on 2 paper marshmallows.

Never tried it—Glue on 1 paper marshmallow.

TEC61092

Mitten Patterns

Use with "Warm Up With a Good Book!"
on page 32.

TEC61092

TEC61092

TEC61092

TEC61092

Candy Patterns
Use with "Sweets for Sale" on page 36.

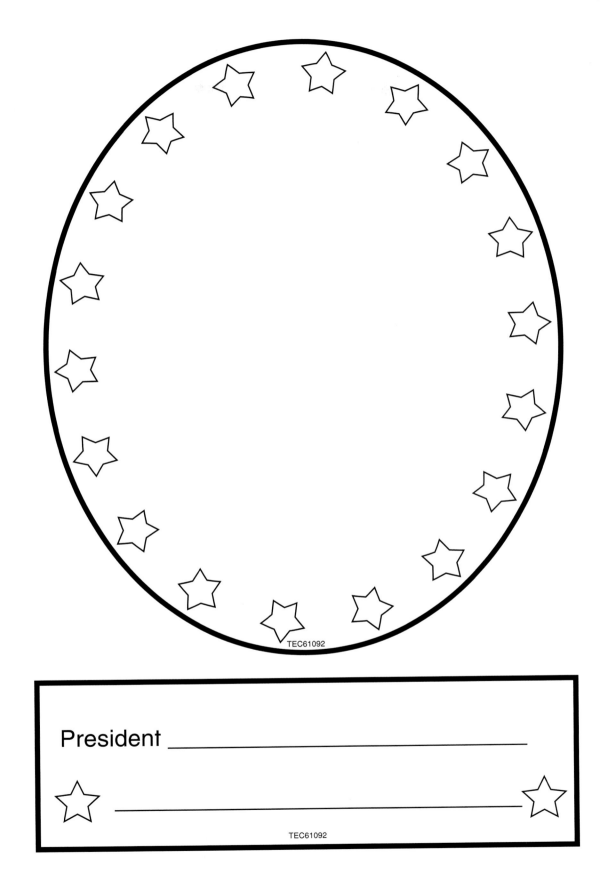

TEC61092

President _____

_____

TEC61092

Tooth Patterns
Use with "Dental Dos, Dental Don'ts" on page 37.

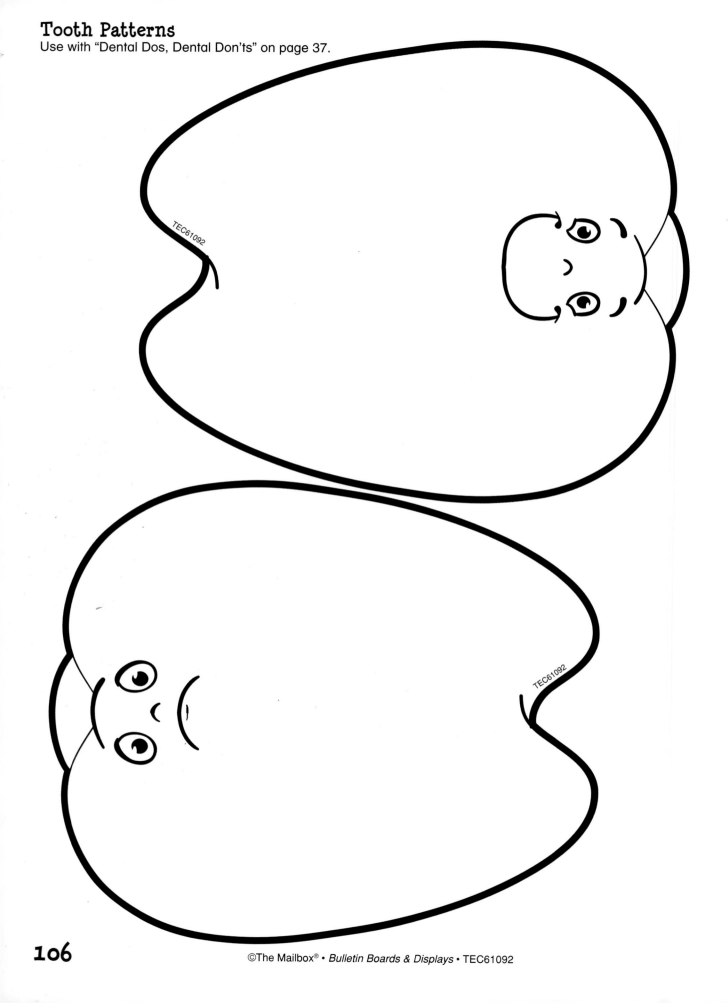

TEC61092

Hat Pattern
Use with "A Hatful of Favorite Books!" on page 40.

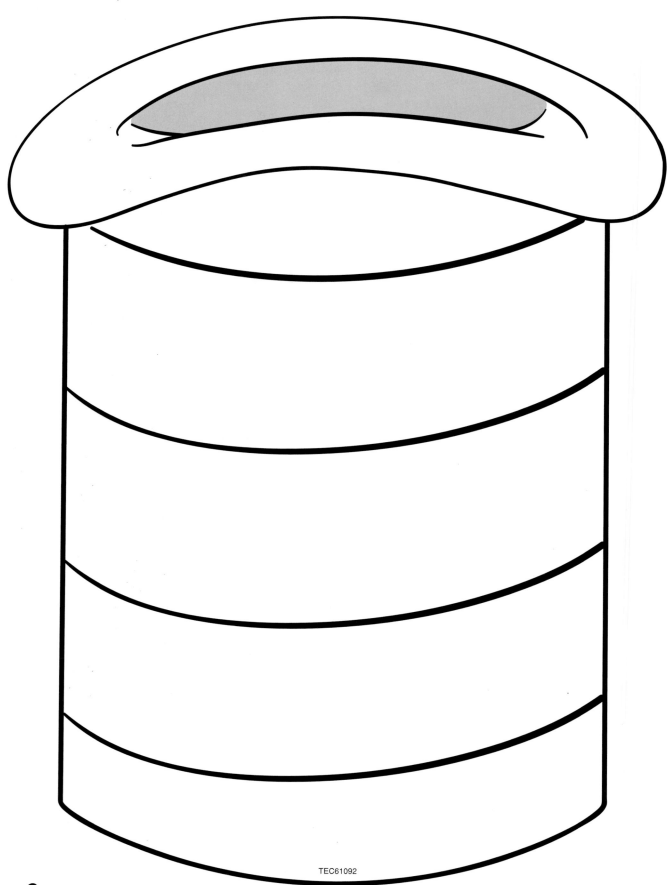

TEC61092

Rabbit Pattern

Use with "Farmer Rabbit's Carrot Patch" on page 41, "Spring Words" on page 42, and "Growing Flower Families" on page 47.

TEC61092

Carrot Pattern
Use with "Farmer Rabbit's Carrot Patch" on page 41.

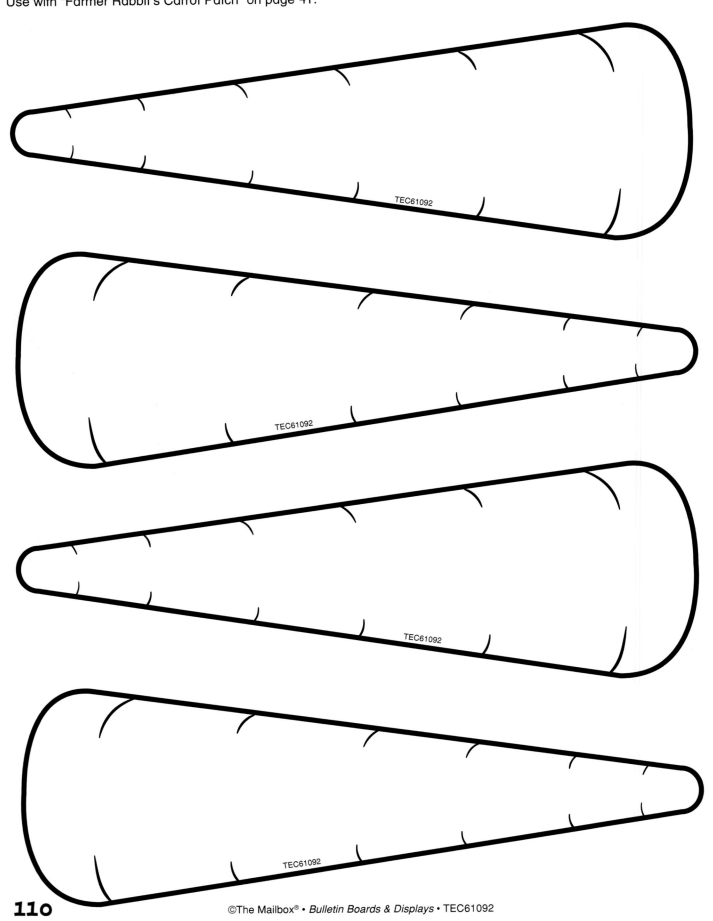

TEC61092

TEC61092

TEC61092

TEC61092

TEC61092

Raindrop Pattern
Use with "April Showers!" on page 43.

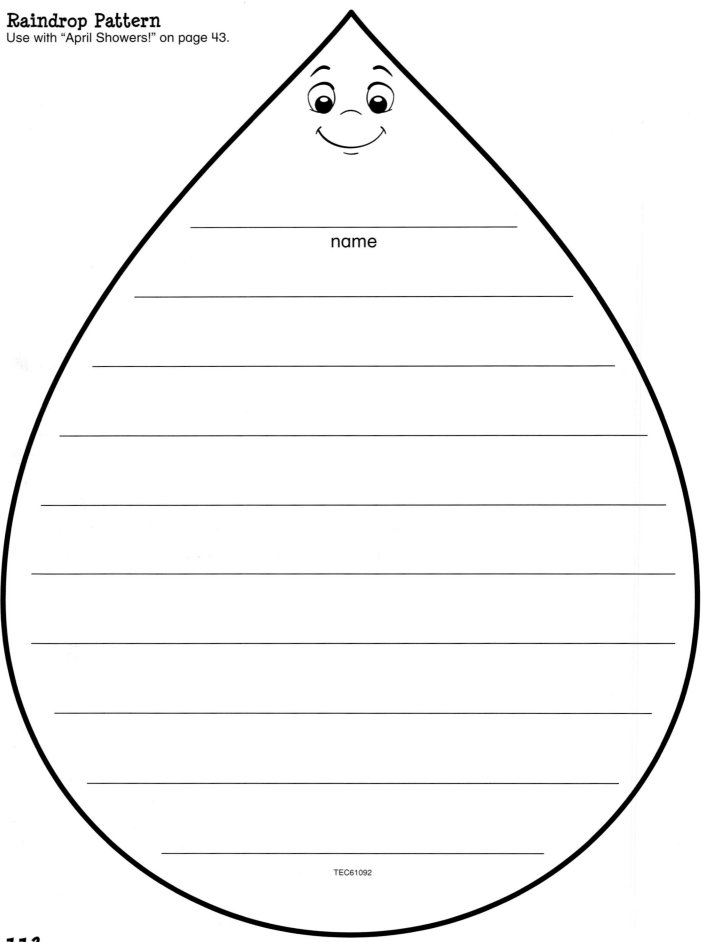

name

TEC61092

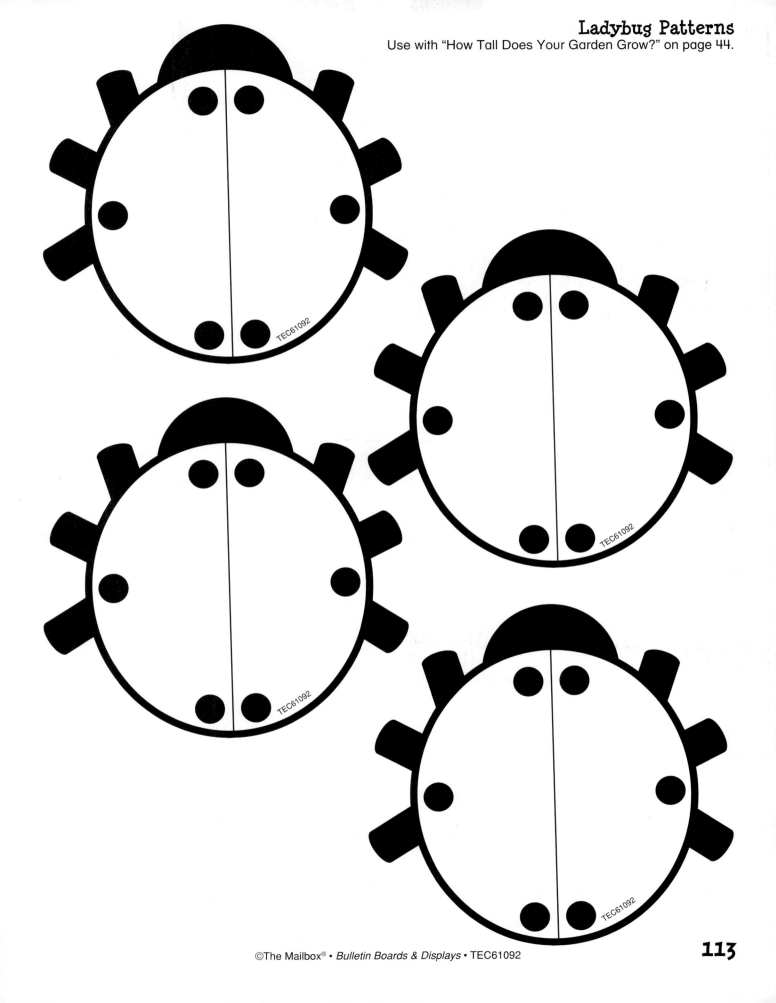

TEC61092

TEC61092

TEC61092

TEC61092

Duck Pattern
Use with "Just Ducky!" on page 45.

Chick Pattern
Use with "Pick a Chick!" on page 45
and "Cracking Into a New Day!"
on page 72.

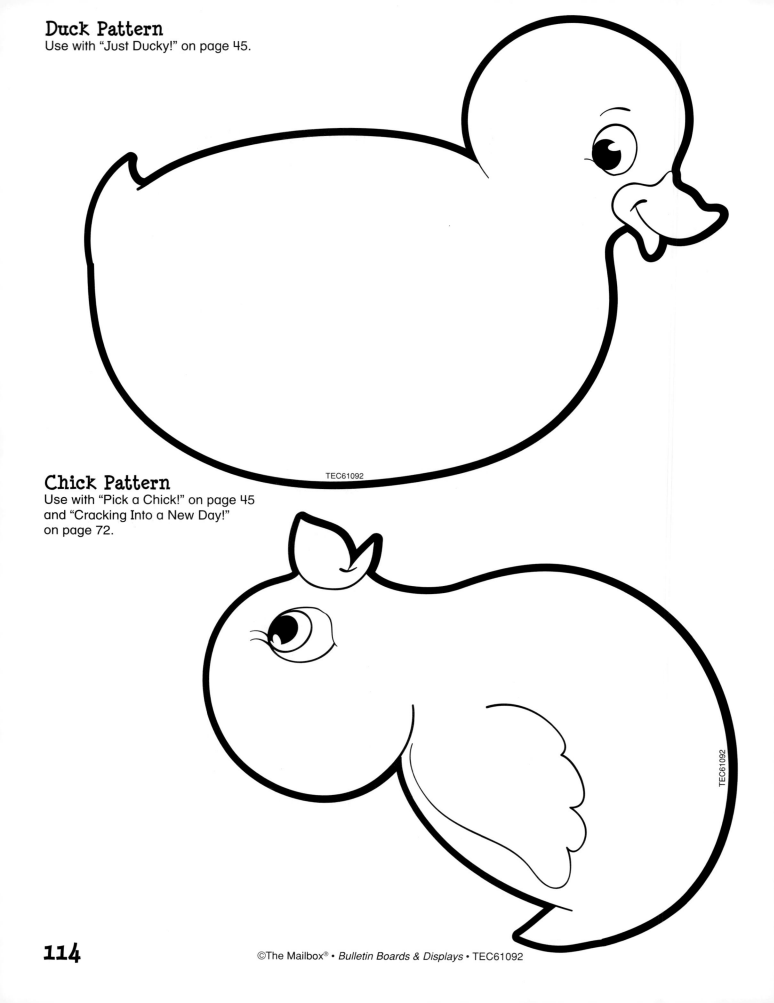

TEC61092

TEC61092

Flower Pattern
Use with "Growing Flower Families" on page 47.

TEC61092

Baseball Buddy Pattern
Use with "We're a Winning Team!" on page 47.

TEC61092

Bee Patterns

Use with "'We're as Busy as Bees!" on page 48 and "What's Buzzing in First Grade?" on page 72.

TEC61092

TEC61092

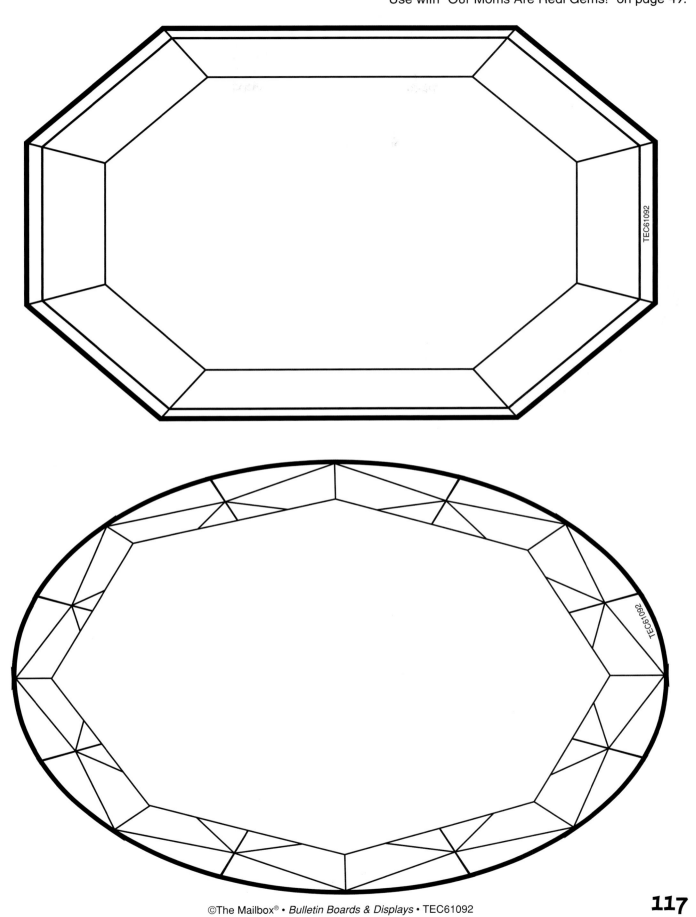

TEC61092

TEC61092

Strawberry Patterns

Use with "Welcome to Our Patch!" on page 7 and "Strawberry Synonyms" on page 49.

TEC61092   TEC61092

Ice Pop Pattern

Use with "Ms. Chapman's Sweet Treats!" on page 50.

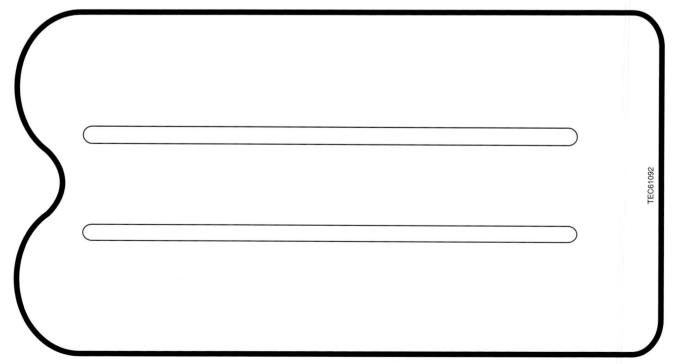

TEC61092

118

TEC61092

Name _____

First grade was a blast!

I learned

_____

_____

_____

©The Mailbox® • *Bulletin Boards & Displays* • TEC61092

Note to the teacher: Use with "Going Out With a Bang!" on page 52.

119

Racecar Patterns

Use with "And They're Off to Second Grade!"
on page 53, "Students, Start Your Engines!"
on page 67, and "A Winning Circle of
Helpers" on page 71.

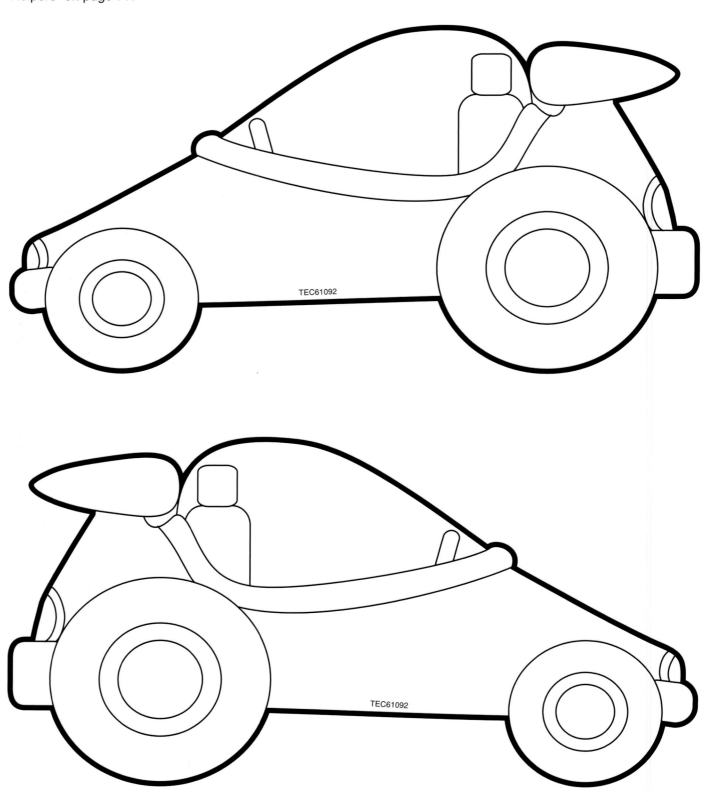

TEC61092

TEC61092

TEC61092

Rocket Pattern

Use with "Blast Off Into 2nd Grade!" on page 54.

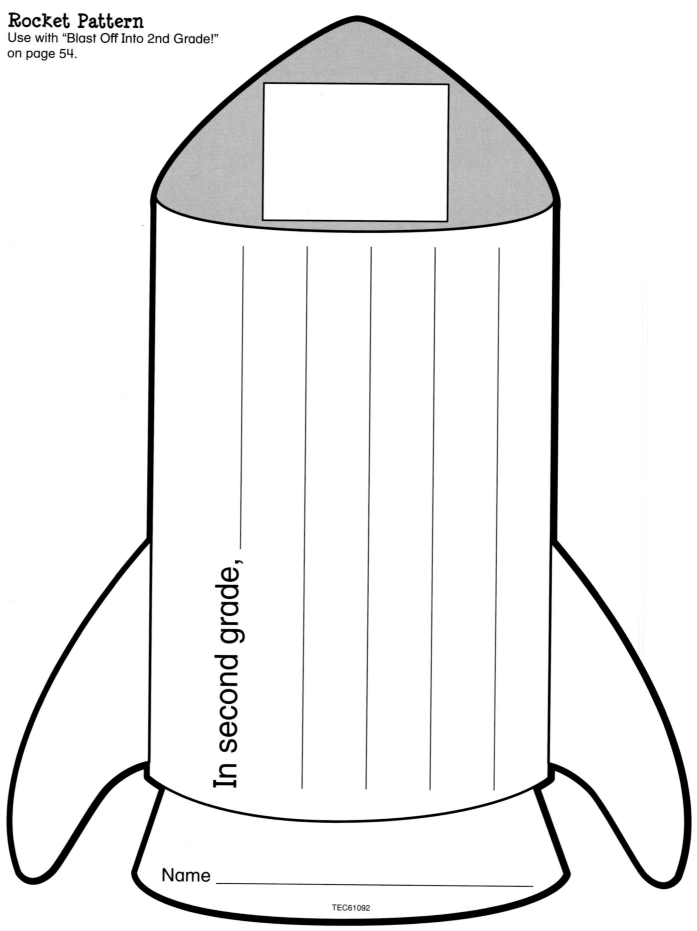

In second grade,

Name _____

TEC61092

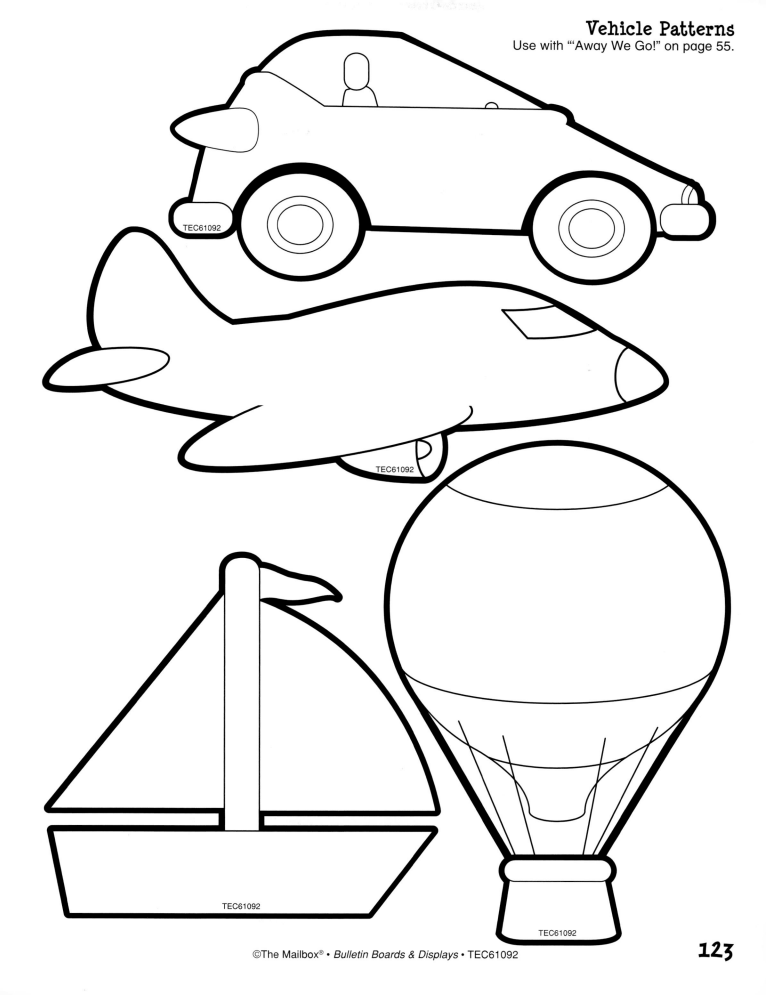

TEC61092

TEC61092

TEC61092

TEC61092

Writing Pattern
Use with "Freshly Squeezed Favorites!" on page 56.

Name _____

First-Grade Favorites

The thing I liked most about first grade was

_____

_____

I think you will like first grade because _____

_____

_____

Paper Topper Pattern
Use with "Star-Spangled Work!" on page 56.

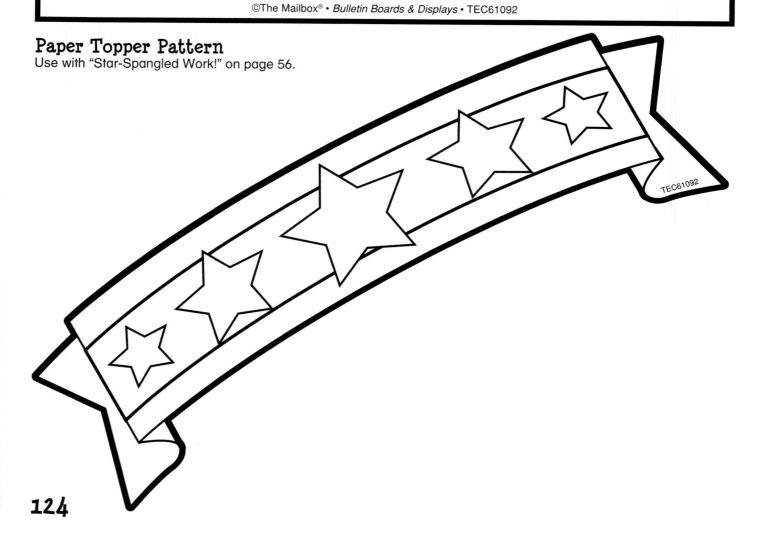

TEC61092

124

TEC61092

Elephant Strips
Use with "Elephant Express" on page 63.

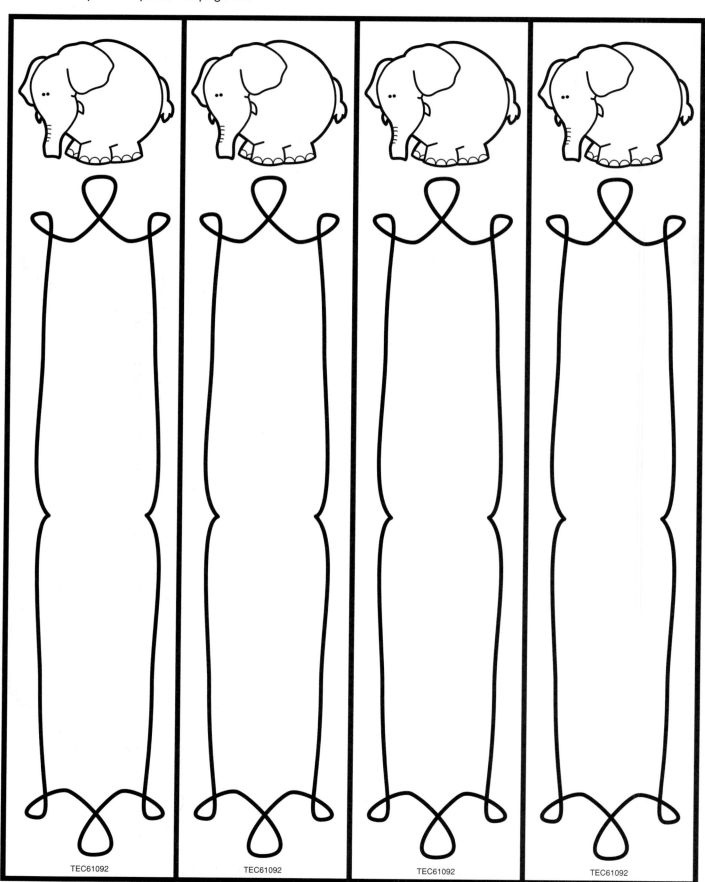

TEC61092   TEC61092   TEC61092   TEC61092

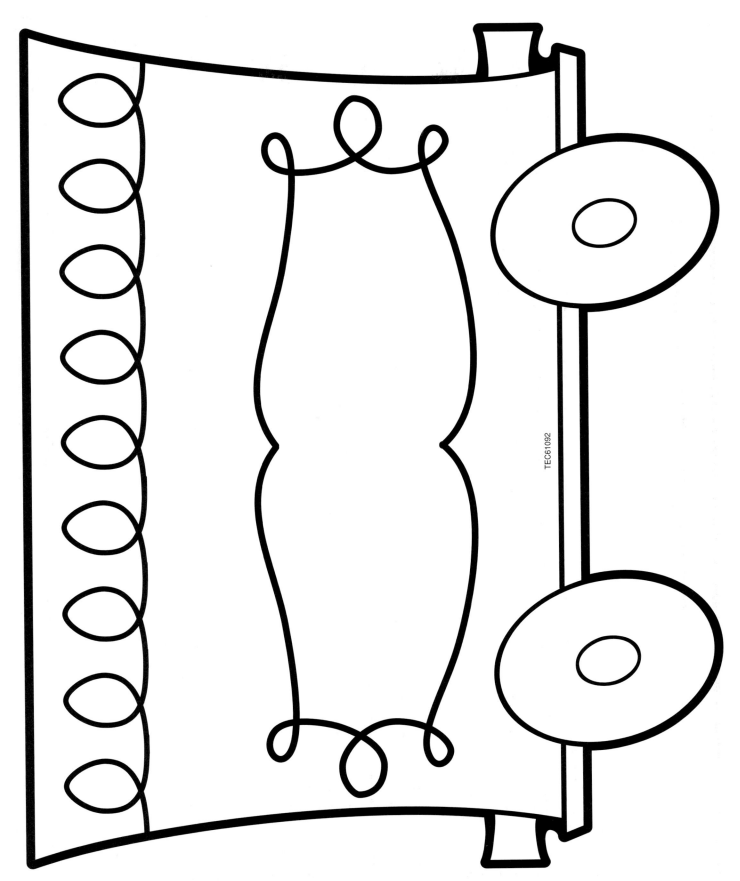

Puzzle Piece Pattern
Use with "Are You Through?" on page 64.

TEC61092

TEC61092

TEC61092

Arm and Leg Patterns
Use with "We Are Full of Good Work!" on page 66.

132

TEC61092

Pirate Pattern
Use with "Work to Treasure!" on page 67.

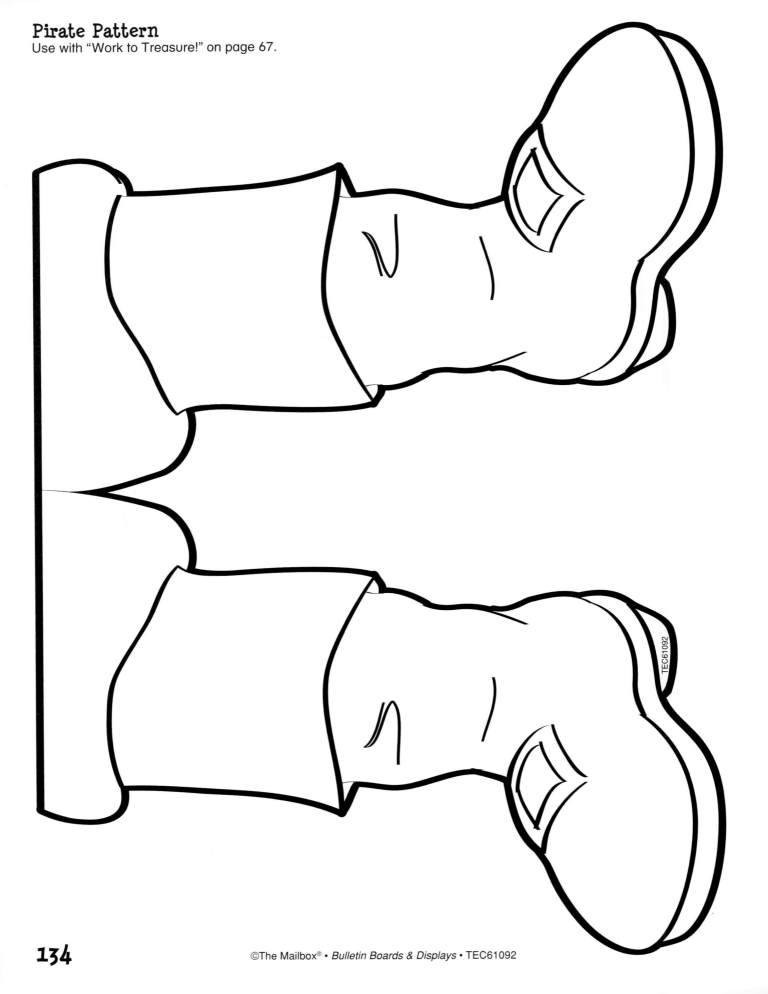

TEC61092

Lightbulb Patterns
Use with "We Are Making Bright Choices!" on page 69.

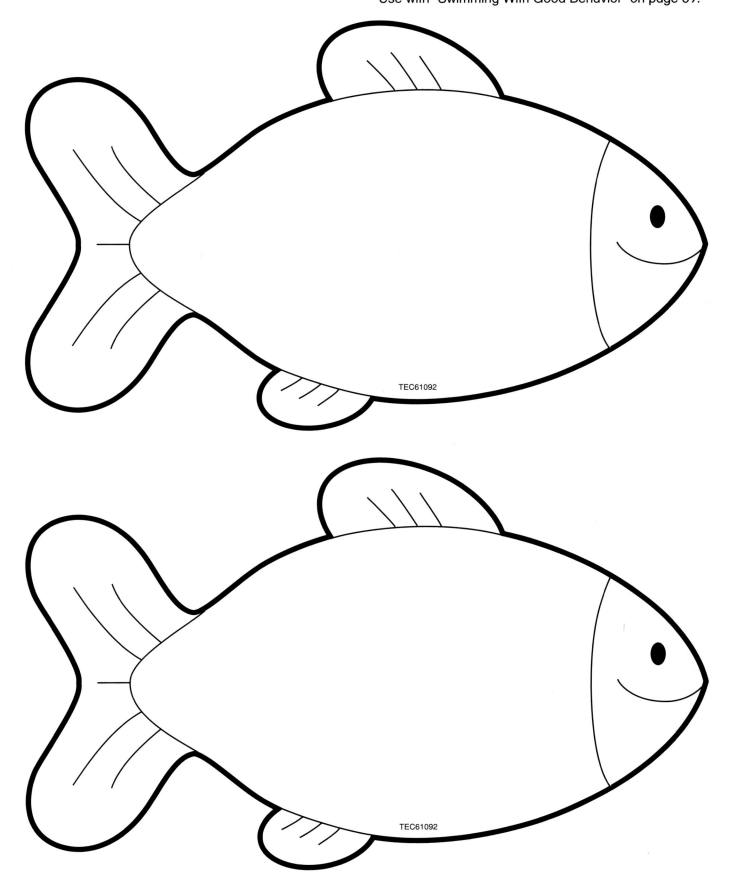

TEC61092

TEC61092

Pig Patterns

Use with "Banking on Good Behavior" on page 70.

TEC61092

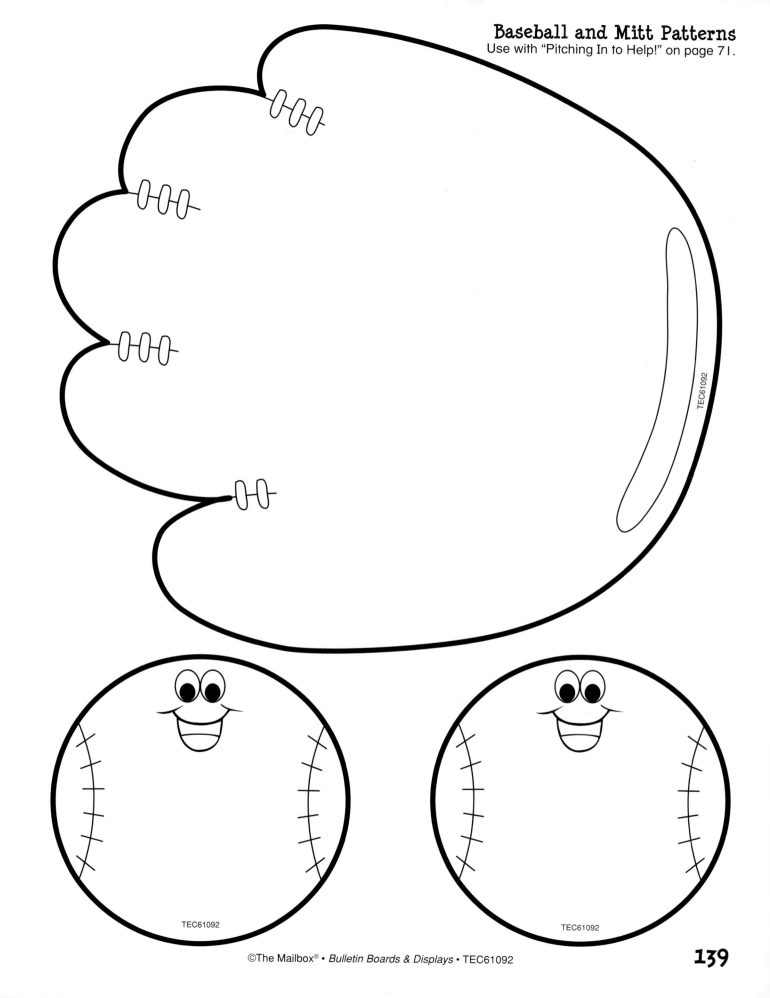

TEC61092

TEC61092

TEC61092

Beehive Pattern

Use with "We're as Busy as Bees!" on page 48
and "What's Buzzing in First Grade?" on page 72.

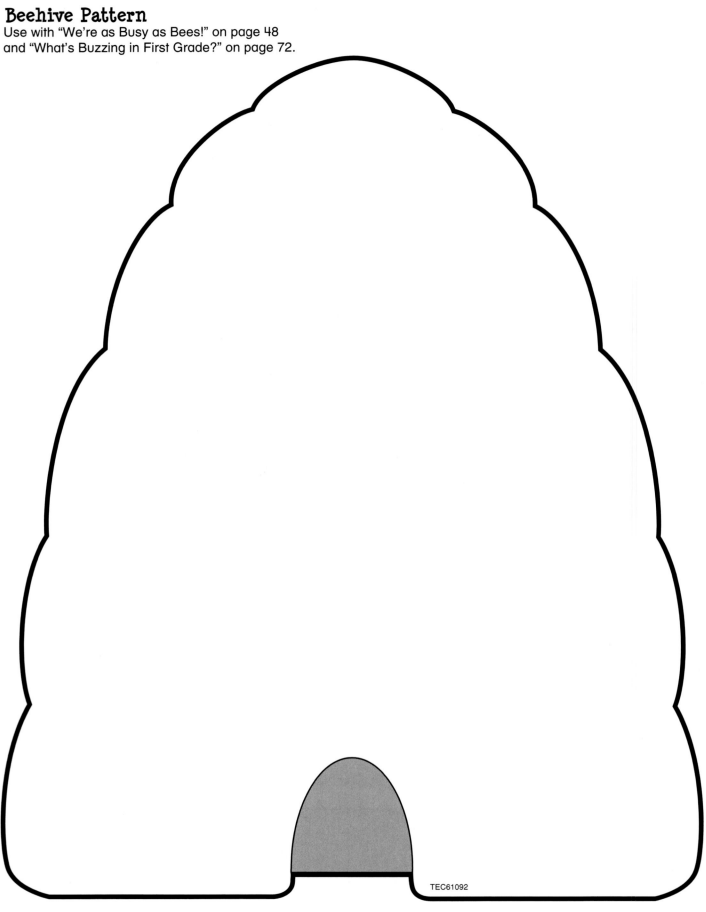

TEC61092

TEC61092

Index

Pattern Index